ROY CA

ON T

ROY CASTLE
ON TAP

His unique tap dancing course

David & Charles

Newton Abbot · London · North Pomfret (Vt)

British Library Cataloguing in Publication Data

Castle, Roy
    Roy Castle on tap: his unique tap
    dancing course.
    1. Tap dancing
    I. Title
    793.3'24   GV1794

    ISBN 0-7153-8869-X

Text and illustrations © Roy Castle 1986
First published 1986
Second impression 1987

Photography by Julian Clode,
The Photographic Training Centre, Earl's Court

Typeset by Typesetters (Birmingham) Ltd,
Smethwick, West Midlands
and printed in Great Britain
by Butler and Tanner Ltd, Frome
for David & Charles Publishers plc
Brunel House   Newton Abbot   Devon

Published in the United States of America
by David & Charles Inc
North Pomfret   Vermont 05053   USA

CONTENTS

Introduction   7

Preparing to Tap   8

Temporary Taps	8	Half Rubber Soles	12
Clothing	8	Mirrors	12
Tap-dancing Surfaces	9	Fitness	12
Shoes and Taps	10	Warm-up	13
Fixing Taps	10		

Basic Steps   14

The Shuffle	14	The Heel	19
The Pupple	16	The Hop	19
The Toe	17	The Catchback	20
The Dig	17	The Brush	21
The Down	18		

Combining Steps   22

Time Step	22	Tune suggestions	34
Time-step Break	24	Hotch	36
Double Time-step	24	Time Hotch Step	37
Triple Time-step	26	Da-pupple-ca	38
Cahito	28	Brush-plus	40
Cahito Tip	30	Shunt	44
Shim Sham	32	Turns	46
Shim Sham Cahito	34	Repeats	50
Thirty-two Bars	34	Alpha-beat Routine	52

Further Steps 56

Tapioca	56	Dig-toe-ca-toe	82
Heel-kick (Hik)	60	Cutaway	83
Cramp Roll	62	Cutaway-ca	85
Flam	64	Double-ca	86
Trenches	65	Extra Heel	88
Pu-he-pl	68	Hand-claps	90
Pu-he-pl Time-step	70	Walking Steps	92
Wing	72	Four-side	94
Double Wing	74	Hupple	96
Pendulum Wing	75	Shuffle-off-to-Buffalo	97
Side-klik	76	Dig-drag	100
Slurp	78	Gallop	102
Jump-o-foot	80	Arm-clocks	104

Routines 106

Soft Shoe	106	Close Beat Feat	132
Three Beat Treat	118	Flambée	136
Time-step Saga	124		

Final Tips 144

INTRODUCTION

Tap dancing is extremely rewarding in many, many ways. First of all, it's fun from the very first lesson. It is a marvellous way of exercising at all levels from 'gentle' to 'violent' and each stage can be equally gratifying and entertaining. Many tap dancers are still able to perform in their seventies or even eighties. Indeed I have taught a seventy-year-old beginner who made amazing progress. He was already a proficient ballroom dancer and could handle some of the 'modern stuff' but had always fancied tapping from being a boy. A fine time to start, but start he did . . . and made remarkable progress, becoming quite a talking point in my school. Stand him next to a three year old and there you have it . . . almost anyone, with effort and enthusiasm, can tap dance.

This book is intended to take you from the very basics of tap, to the point where you will not be afraid to take the awesome step of joining a local tap school. Most people would love to 'have a go' but are scared of either looking silly or holding the others back. The first part of this book should conquer any of those fears and get you over the stumbling start in the private seclusion of your own environment. To help you practise, there are available special tuition cassettes for all routines contained in this book (see page 34).

Once we have got you moving nicely and understanding the basic steps, we put them together into easy routines that can be performed for your own enjoyment, at parties or even local concerts. The routines can be danced solo, double or in groups.

Finally, we shall cover the more advanced steps, together with a few of my own acquired-over-the-years tips and personal discoveries.

Throughout this book, the most important message to you is to enjoy your tapping, and let others enjoy it too.

Temporary Taps

At the very start of your tap dancing exploration, equipment requirements are nil. All you need is enough room to swing your foot. The basic movements are very simple and can be tested without any expense at all. As you gain a little confidence, you will naturally want to get the real feel and exciting sound of the tap. Then you can make a small purchase. All you need at this stage is a set of taps; a pair for the toes and a pair for the heels. No need to go in for a special pair of tap shoes just yet. Most dancing schools can provide taps or recommend a place of purchase. When choosing your first set of taps, pick some light-weight ones as they are easier to stick to the soles of your ordinary shoes as a temporary measure.

For this, use some double-sided sticky pads, obtainable from most stationers. (Carpet tape is also very good.) Make sure that the soles and heels of your shoes are *dry* and *clean*. This is most important. Fix the sticky pads to the inside of the tap, usually three pads per tap, peel off the protective paper and place carefully in the exact position on the shoe and press firmly together.

The tip of the toe tap should be as close as possible to the toe end of the shoe. It is not a good idea to have the tap sticking out.

If you have done a good job attaching the taps, they should stay on for a good session or two, and can easily be removed to return your shoes back to normal. Needless to say, the taps can be used many times by just cleaning off the old sticky pads and replacing them with new ones.

Clothing

The choice of clothing is entirely up to the individual; it is possible to tap dance in almost any outfit. At first, the dancing should not get you into too much of a lather. As you progress, you may find it beneficial to have a change of clothing after an energetic work-out, but this will all become quite obvious to you in the course of time.

When clothing is too baggy (*Fig 2*) you are inclined to lose line and style but, apart from this, there are no hard and fast rules. *Be comfortable!*

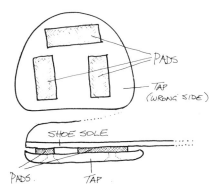

Fig 1 **Attaching the taps**

Fig 2 **Clothes too baggy**

Hardboard is cheap and
effective on kitchen floors
and thin-pile carpets, though
the old-fashioned tap mat is
easily rolled up and more portable

Using a tap mat on thin-pile carpet

Close-up of a tap mat

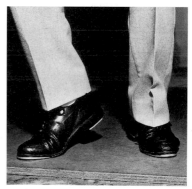

Blockboard can be used on
thick-pile or lumpy carpet

Tap-dancing Surfaces

One difficulty the tap dancer faces is a place to practise. This problem varies with each individual. The lucky student has a nice hard, spacious surface in the house where scuff marks don't matter. These are ideal circumstances enjoyed, alas, by few. Most home situations provide a hard kitchen floor and little else. This, fortunately, is enough for the beginner to reach at least the standard of confidence to join a school and enjoy surface, space, and, may I add, the enthusiasm of others.

Should the kitchen floor take exception to being scratched, there are a few other possibilities.

One of the cheaper ways is to use a piece of hardboard (tapping on the smooth side). This can be obtained in various sizes, the larger the better. Try to avoid having too many joins as they are apt to part slightly and cause you to trip. Hardboard is best on a bare floor but is also quite effective on thin-pile carpets. It is not so good on thick-pile or lumpy carpets. Blockboard is more substantial for thicker carpets but is bulkier, heavier and more difficult to store.

The old-fashioned tap 'mats' are scarce and a trifle expensive but are easily rolled up and put away. Should you happen to be or know a clever woodworker, I show here a photograph of a tap mat. The size can be fashioned according to your personal requirements.

Shoes and Taps

When you are finally convinced that you can tackle tap dancing, it is time to purchase some permanent tap shoes. You must first of all decide whether you are going to get complete, already assembled tap shoes or buy shoes of your choice and fix your own taps.

If you choose 'ready mades', avoid the ones where the taps are riveted to the soles. These are often quite cheap and inviting but they seldom give you the real satisfying tap sound. They are little better than a tapless shoe. The taps need to be adjustable so that you can 'tune' them to your liking.

The female shoe needs an extra decision . . . the size of heel. Very high or stiletto heels are not recommended for obvious reasons. Sprained ankles are *not* the tap dancer's favourite companions – not to mention the ruined kitchen floor. A reasonably raised heel is acceptable if you wish, but you need a wide enough base to accommodate a fair-sized heel tap.

The best taps I have discovered up to the time of this publication are 'Capezio'. They have a lining between tap and shoe which helps the fixing as well as the sound.

If you feel that you could fix your own taps to the shoes of your choice, I have a method I learned from a fantastic old tapper called Fred Brand. He was a great performer and extremely helpful to the raw, wide-eyed youngster, eager to learn everything he could about the Business.

When choosing your shoes, my advice is to concentrate on comfort. You need to be able to tap without forever tending to blisters or cramped feet. I recommend shoes that will be big enough to accommodate an added cushion sole if there is not one already. I cannot stress comfort enough. Sore feet will not only curb your enthusiasm and enjoyment, but hinder your progress. You would also be wrong to get shoes that were too loose and sloppy; and you must choose a happy medium between shoes that are too solid and clumsy and those which are too flimsy. The latter will quickly fall apart and you will have to go through the process of tap fixing too often. The soles of the shoe need to be thick enough to take a short fixing screw. Many modern soles are made out of plastic of one kind or another, which should not be a problem. Leather soles are ideal providing they are not too thin.

Fixing Taps

When buying taps to be fitted permanently, it is most important that they should match the shape of the toe and heel of the shoe as neatly as possible. If the tap is too wide for the shoe, there will be dangerously sharp protrusions sticking out at each side. First and worst, you can easily nudge you own ankles with the unnecessary overlaps; and secondly, anyone dancing alongside is in danger of becoming victim to the slicing machine! Stockings, shoes, trousers etc, are all threatened by over-large taps. If you are unable to get the perfect match, a slightly smaller tap is acceptable and safe.

Should the best available tap be fractionally large, it is possible to file away the offending area. Take care not to file away the upper part of the shoe. The best way is to mark the unwanted area and file it off in a vice.

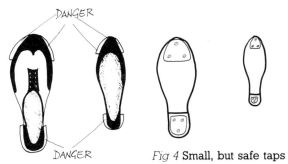

Fig 3 **Taps too big**

Fig 4 **Small, but safe taps**

Fig 5 **Taps too thin**

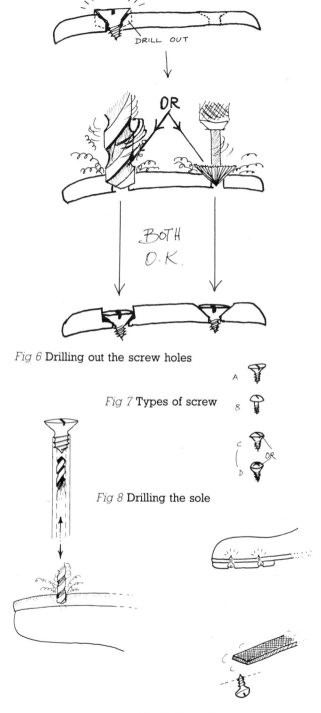

DRILL OUT

OR

BOTH
O.K.

Fig 6 **Drilling out the screw holes**

Fig 7 **Types of screw**

A

B

C

D OR

Fig 8 **Drilling the sole**

Fig 9 **Filing off intrusive points**

Having chosen the shape of your tap, you may also have to choose the ideal thickness. This is also quite an important decision. If the tap is too thin, you will not have much room for screw adjustment. Choose a tap that has enough thickness to allow the screw holes to be enlarged or drilled out a little (*Fig 6*). If the tap is thick enough in itself, but the countersinking is not deep enough to let the tap 'nestle', it will be necessary to drill a little more out of the screw holes.

Another important decision is the type of screw. The usual one is the flat head (*Fig 7a*). This is acceptable, but if it works a little loose it can dig into the floor, causing a fair amount of damage in no time at all and hindering your dancing. The preferable types of screw are the round-headed ones (*Figs 7b, c and d*). Even in the event of them working loose, they don't dig up your kitchen or someone else's beautiful dance floor. The best of these are the ones that are shaped to fit a countersunk hole (*Figs 7c and d*).

To fix the taps, position the tap and mark the hole placings. The toe of the tap *must* match up *exactly* with the toe end of the shoe – not beyond it, not short of it, but bang on! Some taps have three fixing holes, some have four. Both are fine. Hold the tap tightly in the *exact* place on the shoe sole and mark the hole positions with a sharp pencil or pointed object. You must be sure to mark the exact centre of each hole.

Next, bore a hole in each of these marked places. The drill must be thinner than the screw to be used. Only drill a little way into the sole, not all the way through (*see Fig 8*).

Having drilled the holes for one of the taps, it is a good idea to try fitting it. Drive the screws home *very carefully!* The very second you feel the screw tighten up, *stop* – or you will strip the thread and lessen the purchase power of the screw. If, at this stage, the screw head is still 'proud' of the tap, it will be necessary to countersink the holes in the tap a little more (as in *Fig 6*). Be careful not to drill all the way through the tap or it will drop off!

Once you have got the screw placed perfectly within the tap, you may find the point of the screw has penetrated the sole of the shoe inside. Ouch! No matter – we attend to the trespasser with either a file or a hacksaw (*Fig 9*).

Now the fixing screw should be perfect. Follow the same procedure for all four taps. Heels are normally easier. One problem you may have to watch out for is hitting a nail that is an integral part of the shoe. Try to avoid it or drill through it.

When the taps are all in place and 'sitting comfortably', it's time to try them out. Tap around for a while and keep checking them. Gradually they will loosen up a little. If they work too loose and rattle when you shake your foot in the air, they need to be tightened, very gently – don't strip the thread. The perfect tuning is slightly loose without the rattle. You don't want to sound like a wedding car with tin cans trailing. I avoid the 'jingle' type taps for this very reason. You are not in command of rattling taps. When you effect a tap beat, you want to have 'meant' it!

Once you have got your taps finely tuned, you will want them to stay that way. The old-fashioned wrinkle was to put wet salt in with the screw and let it corrode in the leather sole thereby creating a bond. These days, with such sophisticated fixatives around, the salt routine is just a piece of history.

When you are completely satisfied with the tension (it may take a few days or a few hours, depending on how much dancing you do), I suggest a little 'permanency'. Take out the screws and remove the taps (to avoid getting glue on them). Very carefully, with the end of a matchstick or cocktail stick, put a *tiny* blob of glue (eg Araldite Rapid) in the screw holes of the shoe. Replace the taps and screws. Do not get glue on the taps or they will stick to the soles of the shoe and lose their tuning.

I do have one more tip for the 'ultra' enthusiast. In order to get an extra resonant tap sound, we used to cut out a piece of old tin can to the shape of the tap, slightly smaller (to avoid sharp edges sticking out). Drill holes to match the holes in the tap and fit the tin between the tap and shoe. Again, tighten them sufficiently to avoid the rattle.

If you get 'Capezio' taps, fixing instructions are included.

Half Rubber Soles

Tap dancing can sometimes be hampered by slippery surfaces or even slippery shoes. There is a fairly simple way to make sure you can keep your feet on most floors. Rubber stick-on soles are available in many shoe shops or department stores. All you have to do is cut away the toe end to fit up to the tap, then stick them on in the normal way. Instructions and fixing materials are normally supplied with the soles. Should the rubber soles ever get a little slippery after a lot of dancing, either a wipe over with a damp cloth or a rub over with a rough file or coarse sandpaper should return them to their original state.

Mirrors

Mirrors are not absolutely essential, but if you can get a look at yourself, it often improves your posture and helps you to stop looking down at your feet.

The early part of your tap dancing does not rely too heavily on posture, unlike ballet or modern where line is all important. You first of all need to master the basic steps in order to be able to join in, then your style will develop fairly quickly.

If you do not have a mirror, try to share your attention between checking that your feet are doing the right thing, then memorising the feel and performing the step again whilst looking out at your imaginary audience. It is important to know what your feet are doing without having to keep an eye on them!

Fitness

Unlike many other physical pursuits, it is not imperative to be ultra-fit. It *is* possible to tap dance with a few extra pounds of groceries under the belt. Indeed our own star team of Roly-Polys is the perfect example of successful tapping tanks! However, according to how enthusiastic you

become, you will perform the longer, more intricate routines with greater ease if you only have to carry yourself, and not your 'sweet tooth' as well. This will all happen naturally as you become more involved and want to tackle more athletic routines.

If you are not too interested in the energetic work-outs, there is an abundance of material on the gentler side.

Warm-up

I do advise a little warm-up before each session. It is important to start up all engines before stepping on the accelerator. It can be most annoying to pull a muscle or strain a tendon before you have even 'shuffled'! A little warm-up is never wasted.

Hold on to something that will keep you steady, a chair-back or table.

1 Push one leg out in front until it is off the ground. Circle the toe in a clockwise direction to loosen up the ankle. Now anticlockwise. Do this with each foot in turn, twenty times each way. Make as big a circle as you can.

2 Stand with feet together, holding on to the chair-back or whatever. Slowly rise up on to your toes . . . wait . . . and slowly down. Try not to use your arms to take the weight, only to steady yourself. Keep a straight back. Do this ten times *slowly*.

3 Repeat this move on each foot separately.

4 Knee bend. This time, take a little of your weight with your hands until you feel happy about taking the full strain with your legs. With your feet together, bend the knees gradually, lowering yourself until you are squatting (heels off the floor). This exercise must be done carefully. Don't rush it. You may experience a few cracks and bangs – we all do! Once you have reached the full squat position, bounce a few times and come back up slowly. Keep your head up and back straight throughout this exercise.

5 Now to loosen the Achilles! You need a wall or something to lean against about shoulder height. Put folded arms against the wall and rest your head on them. Place your left foot close to the wall (toe pointing straight forwards). Place your right foot a pace back. The right toe *must* face directly forwards and the right heel *must* be on the ground. You should feel a stretching sensation in the calf muscle. Again, gently does it. Stay there for twenty seconds or so. Whilst you are still in this position, sway the hips slowly forwards and backwards, keeping that heel on the ground. Repeat with the other foot.

6 Head rolling. Roll the head slowly clockwise several times and then repeat anticlockwise.

7 With the shoulders, make circular movements forwards and backwards with arms hanging loosely at your side. Ten times in each direction.

8 The traditional touching of the toes is also important. Feel the back of the thighs stretch gently as you reach down, keeping your back straight. Only reach as far as is reasonably comfortable; don't be embarrassed if you can't actually touch your toes – you will in time.

Now shake it all about, legs, arms, head, etc, like swimmers do just before a race.

You should feel fairly flexible by now so here is your very first tap step to start you on your way.

Fig 10 **Stretching the Achilles tendon. The heel must stay down**

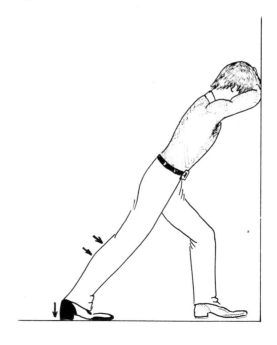

The Shuffle

One of the most important movements in tap dancing is known as the shuffle, a fairly misleading title at first encounter. However, whatever the reason for the name, you will probably use the shuffle more than any other step. There are two movements, simply forward and back. The forward movement resembles kicking a pebble in the street. The foot is picked up, swung forwards, catching the toe on the ground as it swings through. The movement is then reversed and the toe catches the same place on the ground, this time swinging backwards. Throughout this movement, the grounded foot remains still, keeping a steady balance. Try it! Forward . . . back . . . forward . . . back.

At first, all you can really expect from the shuffle is a couple of scraping sounds. With practice, this movement can be shortened, quickened and the beats sharpened into two sweet clicking sounds. As you gain more fine control of your feet, you will be able to 'nod' your toe at the precise split second of impact, thereby achieving a sharper, more explosive sound (*see Fig 12*).

The shuffle can be performed in a straight forward-and-back movement and gradually worked around from twelve o'clock through one, two, three, four and five o'clock with the right foot (*see Fig 13*). Likewise, the left foot can work through 12, 11, 10, 9, 8 and 7 o'clock. Practise harder with the weaker foot so that eventually there will be no such thing as your 'lazy' foot.

Remember to look at your imaginary audience. Don't look down at your feet; let the public watch them! Your job is to make the step look casual, easy and enjoyable. The more you practise, the easier you can make it appear. The shuffle can be a long, slow movement or a very sharp, quick one, and is well worth conquering.

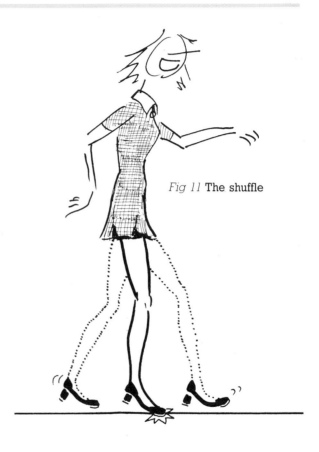

Fig 11 **The shuffle**

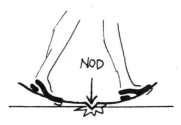

Fig 12 **The nod, showing the toe tap in either direction**

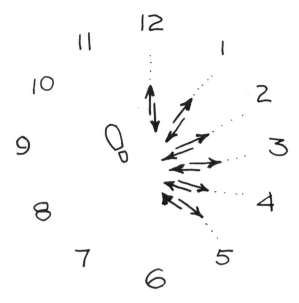

Fig 13 **Practise the shuffle 'round the clock'**

Shuffle at 4 o'clock (*left*) and 9 o'clock

The Pupple

This is simply splitting the shuffle into two parts when it is necessary to use one half of the movement only. On occasions, you will only use the first part of the shuffle, swinging the foot forward, catching the toe but not coming back to complete the shuffle. Many times you will have to follow that forward swing by putting your foot down on the ground a half pace ahead. This is known as 'tap-step' in most dancing schools. On other occasions your foot will be suspended out front and you will need to bring it back, catching the floor along the way, then put it down. This would be a 'catch-step'.

As this book develops, I would like you to get used to a second term for each of these movements which will be a great help when you begin to read my 'tap music'. These extra terms are very simple and will not confuse you.

The two movements of the shuffle are forward and back, or push and pull – 'pushpull'. Take half of each of these words and we have 'pu' and 'pl' or pu'pl as in 'pupple'. Pu'pl means the same as shuffle, but will be more use to you later.

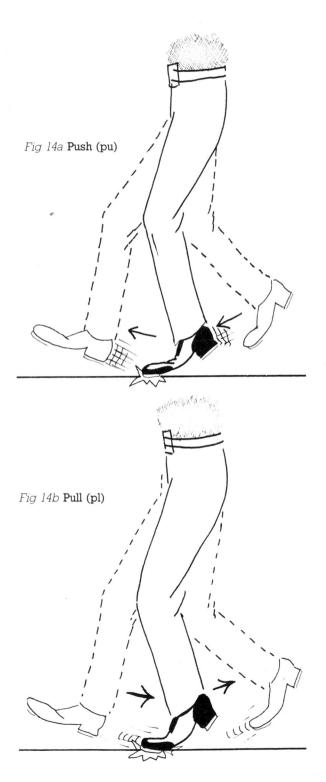

Fig 14a **Push (pu)**

Fig 14b **Pull (pl)**

Strobe photograph of the pu'pl, forwards and backwards, catching toe only

The Toe

This step is always effected from the foot being already suspended. It may be travelling forwards after tapping (pu), or backwards after a pull (pl). You simply put the toe down, keeping the heel raised. This could be followed up by dropping the heel or even hopping on the foot that has 'toe-d'. It is very effective to use the toe step quickly on each toe twice: R L R L, knees relaxed, arms and palms forwards as if holding the crowds back!

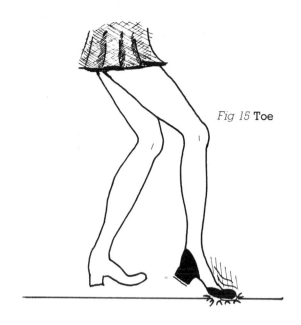

Fig 15 **Toe**

The Dig

I call this the 'tug-o-war' step. The heel is dug into the floor and stops. There are times when the heel is supposed to catch and carry on forwards – this is not one of them! The only forward movement from a 'dig' is to drop the toe as the heel remains in the dig position. This would be known as 'dig-toe' and is used in the soft-shoe routine. When the step is too fast to say dig-toe, abbreviate dig to 'di' and the step becomes di-toe. I am keen to give the name of the step the same rhythm as the step itself; it is then possible to talk the routine as you would tap it.

Fig 16 **Dig**

The Down

This is just a case of putting your foot down! Toe and heel together, in one beat. Not to be confused with 'toe' where the heel remains raised. Down (da) with the right foot then the left foot, keeping the knees a little bent is very Gene Kelly-ish! He can make *so* much out of one da da, keeping his hands forwards like a stand-up piano player. Try it. Nicely bent knees, play the piano, head slightly on one side, smile . . . *da da*!

Fig 17 **Down (da)**

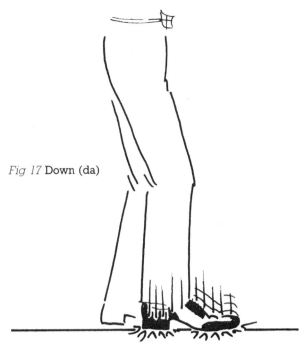

The down, *da da*!

The Heel

Heel is short and sweet. It is simply a drop of the heel from the 'step' or 'toe' position. A good example of the heel beat is to step on to each toe separately, keeping both heels raised, then drop each heel separately, toe, toe, heel, heel. If you use right then left 'toe', keep the same R L order for the heels. Try it both ways. This exercise is also very good for the brain and features in the cramp-roll step.

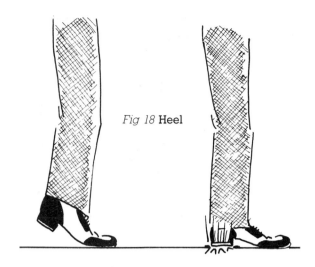

Fig 18 **Heel**

The Hop

The hop is self-explanatory. Whilst one foot is off the ground, you simply jump in the air with the grounded foot and land on the ball of the foot, keeping the other foot suspended. There can be large hops or tiny ones according to the requirements of the routine. A little addition to the hop can be a 'heel'. Hop, land on your toe, drop your heel (two beats). Practise this with both feet. Remember not to look down all the time . . . *smile!*

Fig 19 **Hop**

The Catchback

The catchback (ca) is used in many steps and is an ideal way of 'poaching' a beat whilst stepping back.

You catch the floor with your toe as you step backwards. The preparation for this move is to raise slightly the toe of the working foot and, as you pull it backwards, drop the toe and tap the floor smartly on the way through. The working foot remains suspended behind, awaiting the next command. On most occasions, you will put it straight down behind you, effecting two beats with one backward step. There will be times when you will have to hop on the other foot between the catchback (ca) and putting the working foot down, thereby notching up three beats. There are many ways of incorporating ca, but all in good time . . .

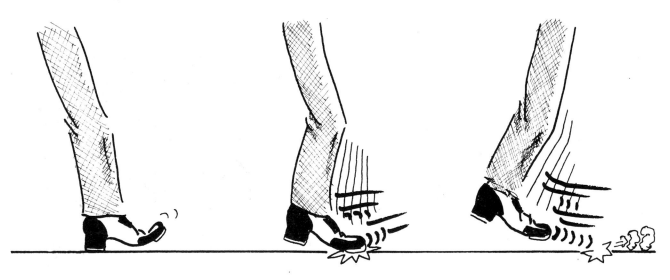

Fig 20 **Catchback (ca)**

The Brush

Brush is the time-honoured term for this particular step. The working foot is raised behind and is swung forward as in the first part of the shuffle (pu). This time, instead of just tapping the toe, the toe *and* heel are slammed into the floor together and continue forwards. The brush normally moves on into a semi-high kick and a hop on the other foot. The brushed foot then comes back to perform the catchback (ca) and is immediately put down (toe). Brush(R), hop(L), ca–toe(R) – four beats. The counting for this is: one, –, two an three; brush, –, Hop-ca-toe.

The arm movements to this step are as important as the feet. As you brush, the hands start together at the belt buckle area, travel upwards past your face, then part company making arcs in outward directions then returning to sides. The arm movement resembles a fountain. Don't be afraid to make this a big move, up and round. The return of the arms to the side should coincide with the last beat of the brush, –, hop-ca-TOE!

Fig 21 **Brush**

Strobe photograph of the brush, showing foot slammed flat down and following through

Time Step

Once you can perform the basic steps, it is a good idea to string a few together. This next section deals with simple, short combinations and introduces the written form of tap.
The three steps we are going to use for our first combination are:
1 Pu'pl (shuffle)
2 Hop
3 Toe

Put them together like this:
1 Pu'pl(R)
2 Hop(L)
3 Toe(R)

You should finish with both toes on the ground, heels raised. Now try it with the other foot:
1 Pu'pl(L)
2 Hop(R)
3 Toe(L)

Keep repeating this until you can tap it with a steady regular rhythm. The main beat is emphasised on the pl of 1 –pu'PL hop toe pu'PL hop toe. If you were counting in rhythm, the timing would be: an ONE an two an THREE an four etc. If you were being counted in, it would go like this: one, two, three, four, an ONE an two an THREE an four an etc. Or one, two, three, four, pu'PL hop toe pu'PL hop toe etc.
Keep this in mind as we add another short combination. This time we use pu-toe and toe:
4 Pu-toe(L)
5 Toe(R)
Also,
4 Pu-toe(R)
5 Toe(L)
These are added to the first combination. Using the numbers 1–5 together, we get:
Pu'pl(R) hop(L) toe(R) pu-toe(L) toe(R) and pu'pl(L) hop(R) toe(L) pu-toe(R) toe(L).

You have now tapped the basic 'time step', the most famous tap dance step of all. The time step to a tapper is as important as the corner-stone to a builder or the canvas to a painter. The time step has many variations, but the basic step is the one on which we build.
It is now time to show you what the time step looks like when it is written down. First, an introduction to the tap 'grid' (*Fig 22*).
Working from the top downwards, the centre 'lane' is for the rhythm count. If the tempo is a nice, steady four beats in a bar, we need to accommodate the half beats also. Four straight beats are: one, two, three, four. When we add the half beats we get: one an two an three an four an. On the grid, we allow for the half beats all the way resulting in a four-beat rhythm using eight squares. When dancing to a waltz (three beats to the bar), we use six squares.
The left lane on the grid is for the left foot and the right lane, for the right foot. It's just a case of getting used to it! Now let's look at our time step. As the hop is the main beat, and is performed on the first beat of the bar, the pu'pl preceding it starts on the 'four an' count of the bar before. So we get 'one an two an three an' for nothing, then we begin.

A Count in. Don't start yet.
B Count in. Don't start yet.
C Count in. Don't start yet.
D Count in. Don't start yet.
E Count in. Don't start yet.
F Count in. Don't start yet.
G Pu (first part of shuffle), right foot. Arrow points direction of tap movement. Name of square: 4.
H Pl (second part of shuffle), right foot. Arrow points direction. Name of square: 4-n.
I Hop on left foot (left 'lane'). First beat of bar. Name of square: 1.
J This time, there is no beat by either foot, so nothing is written in. However, the half beat must be counted even though nothing is happening. The left foot remains on the floor whilst the right foot is still suspended from the pl of square 4-n. Name of this square: 1-n.
K Toe. Put right toe down by side of left. Name of square: 2.
L Pu, left foot. Arrow points direction. Name of square: 2-n.
M Put toe down slightly forward of pu in previous square. This square name: 3.
N Pick up right foot and put toe down. Square name: 3-n.
O From here the step is repeated on the opposite feet: Pu, left foot. Square name: 4.
P Pl, left foot. Square name: 4-n.
Q Hop(R)
R Pause
S Toe(L)
T Pu(R)
U Toe(R)
V Toe(L)
W Pu(R)
X Pl(R) etc. G and H are exactly the same as W and X. This can be danced round and round to any music with four beats to the bar, slowly or, when you get fluent, faster. We can now begin to build on this most important step.

LEFT FOOT	RHYTHM COUNT	RIGHT FOOT	TEMP REF COL
	1		A
	N		B
	2		C
	N		D
	3		E
	N		F
	4	Pu ↗	G
	N	Pl ↙	H
Hop	1		I
	N		J
	2	Toe	K
↖ Pu	N		L
Toe	3		M
	N	Toe	N
↖ Pu	4		O
↓ Pl	N		P
	1	Hop	Q
	N		R
Toe	2		S
	N	Pu ↗	T
	3	Toe	U
Toe	N		V
	4	Pu ↗	W
	N	Pl ↙	X
	Etc		

Fig 22 **Time step**

Time-step Break

Once you can dance the time step fluently, it is in itself rhythmic enough to sustain a chorus of four-beat music. However, it is nice to have something a little different here and there. One step to relieve the monotony is the 'break'. The time step, as we have learned it, is performed twice, once starting with the right foot, then the left. Now we introduce the break. The first part is the same as the time step: Pu'pl(R) hop(L) toe(R). Now the new bit: Pu'pl-toe(L) pu'pl-toe(R) pu'pl-toe(L) toe(R). (*For the grid, see Fig 23a.*)

On the condensed version of the same grid (*Fig 23b*), you will see that:
A indicates the first time step starting on the right foot.
B is the second time step starting on left foot.
C is the break.

This sequence can be repeated without stopping but the feet are reversed. First time step starts on the left. Second on the right. Break starts on the left. You can now continue as from 'A' again. This is called the 'single' time-step with break. Now for the 'double' time-step . . .

Double Time-step

Don't be alarmed at the title. You don't have to double the taps or the tempo. We just add one more beat to the single time-step. The extra beat is put into the pause after the 'hop'. We begin the time step as usual: Pu'pl(R) hop(L). Now, instead of the pause, we add a pu with the right foot before putting the toe down. The new sequence now looks like this: Pu'pl(R) hop(L) pu-toe(R) pu-toe(L) toe(R). The extra pu is added each time after the hop. Have a look at the grid (*Fig 24*).

LEFT FOOT	TIME	RIGHT FOOT	CONTINUED L.F.	TIME	R.F.
	4	Pu↗	Hop	1	
	N	PL↓		N	
Hop	1			2	Toe
	N		↖Pu	N	
	2	Toe	↓PL	3	
↖Pu	N		Toe	N	
Toe	3			4	Pu↗
	N	Toe		N	PL↓
↖Pu	4			1	Toe
↓PL	N		↖Pu	N	
	1	Hop	↓PL	2	
	N		Toe	N	
Toe	2			3	Toe
	N	Pu↗		N	
	3	Toe	↖Pu	4	
Toe	N		↓PL	N	
	4	Pu↗		1	Hop
	N	PL↓		N	
CONTINUE NEXT COLUMN ↗					

Fig 23a **Single time-step with break**

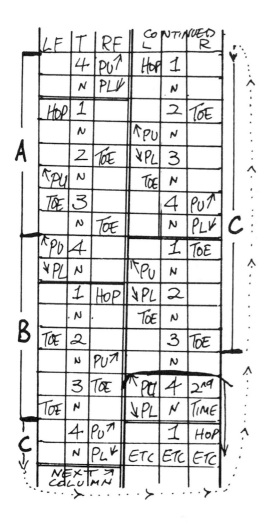

Fig 23b **Single time-step with break**

Fig 24 Double time-step

1

	L	R	
	4	Pu↗	
	N	PL↘	
HOP	1		
	N	**Pu**↗	*NEW*
	2	TOE	
↖Pu	N		
TOE	3		
	N	TOE	
→↖Pu	4	—	
↓PL	N		
	1	HOP	
↖**Pu***	N		
TOE	2		
	N	Pu↗	
	3	TOE	
TOE	N		
—	4	Pu↗	
	N	PL↘	
HOP	1		
	N	**Pu**↗*	
	2	TOE	
↖Pu	N	NEXT COLUMN	

2

	L	R	
↓PL	3		
TOE	N		
	4	Pu↗	
	N	PL↘	
	1	TOE	
↑Pu	N		
↓PL	2		
TOE	N		
	3	TOE	
	N		
↑Pu	4		
↓PL	N		
	1	HOP	
*↑**Pu**	N		
TOE	2		
	N	Pu↗	
	3	TOE	
TOE	N		
	4	Pu↗	
	N	PL↘	
HOP	1		
	N	**Pu**↗*	
	ETC.		

Triple Time-step

For the triple time-step, we turn the newly added pu into a pu'pl. For the single time-step we had a hop followed by a pause. For the double, we followed the hop with a pu; now for the triple we follow the hop with a pu'pl. The pu'pl is a quick one and is better tapped slightly out to the side, around two o'clock for the right foot and ten o'clock for the left.

On the grid, the extra pu'pl has to be written over the 'one an' count, so we have to make this 'one an a' to accommodate three beats in two squares (*Fig 25*). The whole of the triple time-step with the triple break is shown in *Fig 26*.

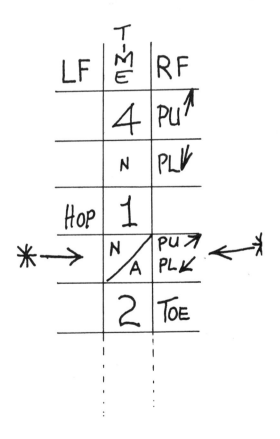

Fig 25 **Triple time-step**

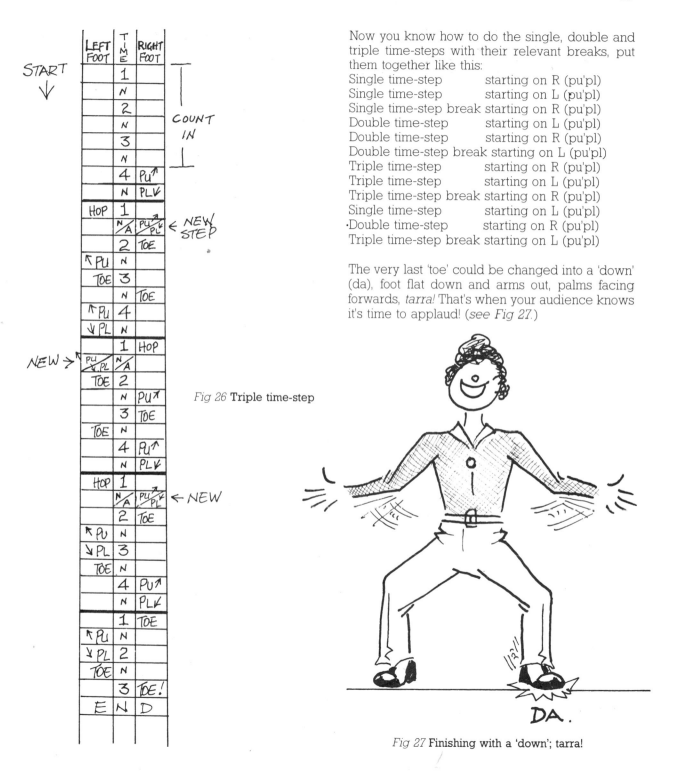

START ↓

LEFT FOOT	TIME	RIGHT FOOT
	1	
	N	
	2	
	N	
	3	
	N	
	4	Pu↗
	N	PL↘
HOP	1	
N/A	N/A	Pu↗/PL↘
	2	TOE
↖PU	N	
TOE	3	
	N	TOE
↖Pu	4	
↓PL	N	
	1	HOP
Pu↗/↓PL	N/A	
TOE	2	
	N	PU↗
	3	TOE
TOE	N	
	4	Pu↗
	N	PL↘
HOP	1	
N/A	N/A	Pu↗/PL↘
	2	TOE
↖PU	N	
↓PL	3	
TOE	N	
	4	Pu↗
	N	PL↘
	1	TOE
↖PU	N	
↓PL	2	
TOE	N	
	3	TOE!
E	N	D

COUNT IN

← NEW STEP

NEW →

← NEW

Fig 26 **Triple time-step**

Now you know how to do the single, double and triple time-steps with their relevant breaks, put them together like this:

Single time-step   starting on R (pu'pl)
Single time-step   starting on L (pu'pl)
Single time-step break starting on R (pu'pl)
Double time-step   starting on L (pu'pl)
Double time-step   starting on R (pu'pl)
Double time-step break starting on L (pu'pl)
Triple time-step   starting on R (pu'pl)
Triple time-step   starting on L (pu'pl)
Triple time-step break starting on R (pu'pl)
Single time-step   starting on L (pu'pl)
·Double time-step   starting on R (pu'pl)
Triple time-step break starting on L (pu'pl)

The very last 'toe' could be changed into a 'down' (da), foot flat down and arms out, palms facing forwards, *tarra!* That's when your audience knows it's time to applaud! (*see Fig 27.*)

DA.

Fig 27 **Finishing with a 'down'; tarra!**

Cahito

Pronounced 'kaheetoe', this is good for a three-beat rhythm. It consists of ca (catchback), he (heel), and toe – cahito, three beats. We will start with the right foot.

The preparation is to raise slightly the R toe keeping the heel down.

1 First beat is a catchback (ca) with the R toe. At the same time as the R ca, raise the L heel in preparation.

2 Drop the L heel. R foot is still suspended, travelling slightly backwards.

3 R foot steps back on toe, keeping R heel raised. At the same time, the L toe is raised, keeping L heel down.

4 We now repeat 1 on opposite feet, ca L toe, keeping R heel raised.

5 Drop R heel.

6 Step back on to L toe and raise R toe for ca(R).
Now you repeat from 1.

This step moves backwards. Take large steps or small ones according to what suits you or the requirements of the routine. The main emphasis is on the 'toe' beat. The arm movements are: Ca(R), left arm forward and right arm back; ca(L) right arm forward, left arm back.

The cahito may seem a little strange at first then, suddenly, you get the idea and it's well worth persevering with it. Once you are cahito-ing easily, try starting off with the 'he' as in he-toe-ca, then with the toe, becoming toe-ca-he. All these variations will be useful to you as you develop routines later.

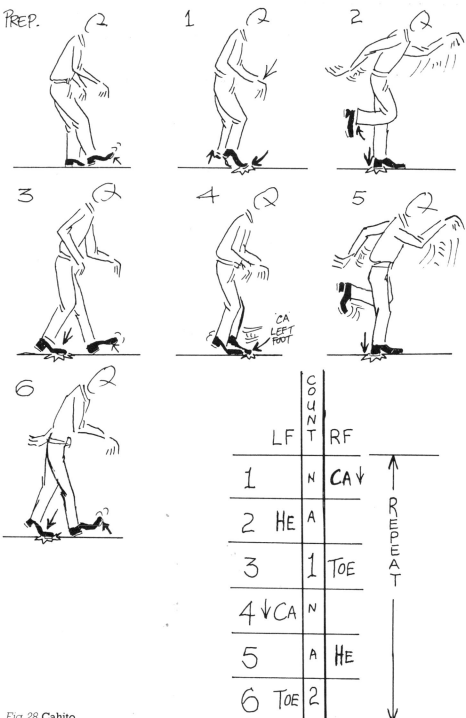

PREP.

1

2

3

4

CA
LEFT
FOOT

5

6

LF	COUNT	RF
1	N	CA↓
2 HE	A	
3	1	TOE
4↓CA	N	
5	A	HE
6 TOE	2	

REPEAT

Fig 28 **Cahito**

Cahito Tip

Now we can add a little more to the cahito. The new step is called 'tip' and is one of the main reasons for having the toe tap fixed flush with the toe of the shoe. The tip is merely a stabbing of the toe into the floor behind you. This movement seldom, if ever, takes the weight. It is just tip and raise (*Fig 29*). Here is how it can be used with the cahito.

As this is a three-beat rhythm, the counting is: 1-n-a-2-n-a-3-n-a-4-n-a. The step starts on the 'a' immediately preceding the first, main beat, '1'. We start with the L heel, followed by toe(R), on the count of '1' as in the cahito/tip grid (*Fig 30*). Note: There is a pause beat after each tip. The cahito/tip grid is repeatable exactly as it stands. From the last 'four an' start again at the top with 'a'. Notice the effect of the tip crossing over at the back, eg right tip across and behind L foot and vice versa (*Figs 31a and b*).

The arm movements for the cahito are as before. When you get to the tip with the L foot, both arms swing right (*Fig 31a*). As you tip with the R foot, both arms swing left (*Fig 31b*).

TIP.

Fig 29 **Tip**

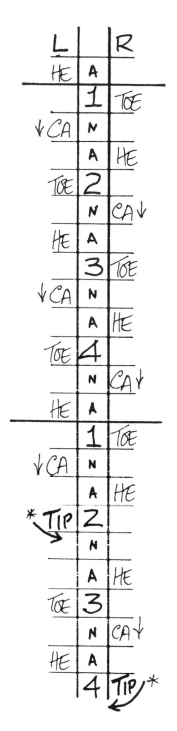

Fig 30 **Cahito with tip**

Fig 31a **Cahito tip (left foot) with arms**

Fig 31b **Cahito tip (right foot) with arms**

Shim sham

One of the great rhythm steps, the shim sham has been handed down through the generations. There is very little movement involved but the feel is most important.

The shim sham (*Fig 32*) is often used when tappers get together for an 'ad-lib' session. All the participants start together doing the shim sham, then each one in turn comes out front and does their 'thing' whilst the others continue providing the background rhythm with the shim sham.

The sound of the step is something like this: AN a one AN a two AN a three bee AN a four. The strong beat is the off beat (AN).

The step goes like this:

1 On the AN, the R foot is slammed down a quarter pace towards one o'clock. Immediately, the same foot prepares for a catchback. (This preparation is not included in the count.)

2 On the 'a' count, catchback with the R foot (leave suspended).

3 On the 'one' count, the R foot is put down in line with the L (toe and heel together as in da or down) – three beats, all with the same foot. In our tap-talk, this is known as da-ca-da, echoing the three beats of the step, but for nostalgia, we will still call this basic step the shim sham.

Putting the whole thing together, we get:

Shim sham(R)
Shim sham(L)
Shim sham(R)
Da(down)(L)
Shim sham(R)

The da on the L foot is a quick one and is the 'bee' of our original counting exercise (AN a three bee AN a four). The chart terms for the steps are:

1 Da(R)
2 Ca(R)
3 Da(R) etc

The whole shim sham is: Da-ca-da(R) da-ca-da(L) da-ca-da(R) da(L) da-ca-da(R). You then repeat the step, starting on the L foot and repeating R and L as long as you like.

We will add to this shortly. In the meantime, *Fig 33a* shows the shim sham grid. The addition at the bottom of the second column is the syncopated rhythm. The ca is slightly held back so that, instead of three equal beats (4 an 1), the feel is 4 an a 1, the 4 being the first da, the 'an' being a pause, the 'a' being the syncopated ca and the 1 being the final da. If we replace the 'an' with a dash, you may get the idea: 4, –, a, 1; or da, –, ca-da. This syncopated feel also applies to the da featured as the 'bee' (*Fig 33b*).

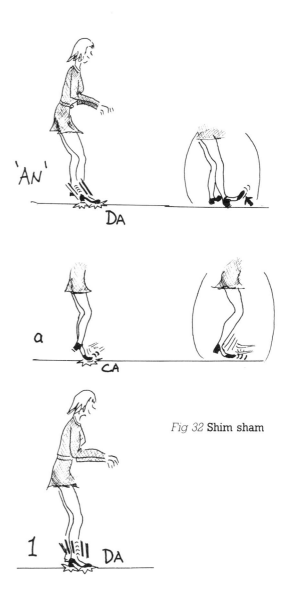

Fig 32 **Shim sham**

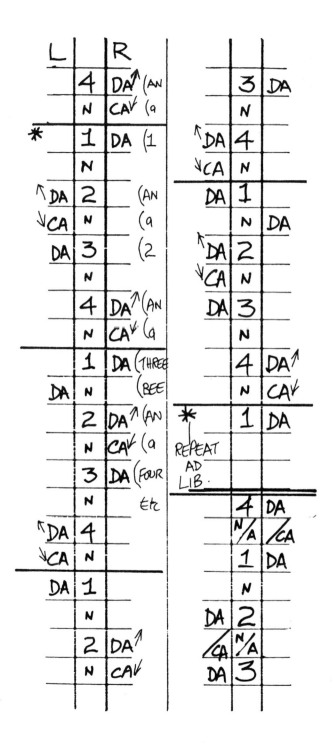

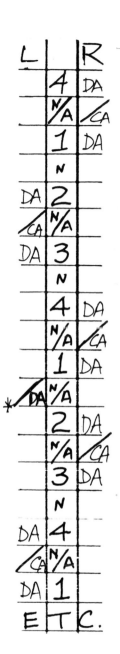

Fig 33b Shim sham with da as 'bee'

Fig 33a Shim sham

Shim Sham Cahito

When we add the cahito to the shim sham, the cahito rhythm takes on a slightly different feel, but is exactly the same step:

Shim sham(R) shim sham(L) shim sham(R) da(L) shim sham(R) shim sham(L) shim sham(R) shim sham(L) da(R) shim sham(L) shim sham(R) shim sham(L) shim sham(R) da(L) da-ca(R) he(L) toe(R) ca(L) he(R) toe(L) ca(R) he(L) toe(R) ca(L) he(R) toe(L) ca(R) he(L) toe(R) ca(L) he(R) DA!(L).

Thirty-two Bars

Now you have reached the standard where you can string a whole chorus together. A normal four-beat tune lasts for thirty-two bars. Multiples of four bars are ideal for the steps we now know. Here is a thirty-two bar routine:
Single time-step with break – four-bars
Double time-step with break – four-bars
Triple time-step with break – four-bars

Single t/s, double t/s, triple t/s, break – four-bars. Total – sixteen-bars. Without a break in the tempo, dance the shim sham routine coupled up to the cahito, twice – sixteen-bars. Grand total – thirty-two-bars.

You will probably get more than one chorus of music so, at this stage, just start the routine again. Keep practising this sequence until you are so confident of the steps that you can 'sell' them. Remember not to look down at your feet. A smiling face is much more attractive than the top of your head.

Tune Suggestions

When dancing the single, double and triple time-steps with breaks, the ideal music is rock n' roll. *Rock around the Clock* fits the time-step sequence perfectly. The average rock n' roll tune lasts for twelve bars: four bars for the single time-step with break; four bars for the double, and four for the triple.

There is also a lot of twelve-bar blues featured in jazz music, a classic example being the main theme in *St Louis Blues*.

One of the all-time greats for the thirty-two bar sequence is *Bye-bye Blues*; it has plenty of open spaces for the taps to be heard easily. Another old timer is *Bye-bye Blackbird*; again, the simplicity of the tune leaves lovely 'gaps for taps'. *Mack The Knife* is also suitable, as one chorus lasts for sixteen bars: at the end of one chorus the time-

step sequence should be completed; at the end of the next chorus the shim sham cahito (repeated) should be complete. Two choruses of '*Mack*' equals 32 bars.

Remember the phrase 'gaps for taps'; it is most important when choosing a tune or record for your routine. An over-orchestrated piece of music leaves no room for the taps to be heard and you are battling away to no avail. Your audience loves to hear the rhythm from your feet – if the music is so involved that it gets in the way, you will confuse the issue and lose impact.

Special tuition cassettes, at performance and practice speeds, for all routines contained in this book are available from:
Ryan Slade International Ltd,
38 Holywell Hill,
St Albans,
Herts AL1 1BU.
Please send a stamped addressed envelope for information.

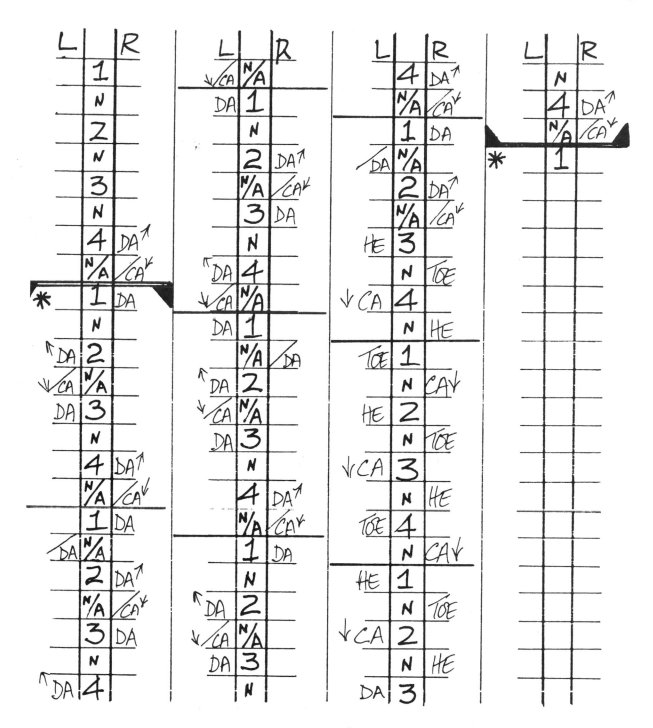

Fig 34 Shim sham cahito

Hotch

Ready for another challenge? The hotch is a mixture of a hop and a catchback. However, for the sake of the grid, it will still be known as 'ca'. The step is like the ordinary ca except it is performed whilst the other foot is off the ground. You will need something to help you keep your balance at first, such as a chair-back, table or anything that will act as a substitute for the dancing class barre. (*see Fig 35.*)

1 Raise one foot behind you. Prepare the grounded foot for the catchback (raise the toe slightly keeping the heel down).
2 Pull the grounded foot back and catch it on the floor (2A); continue following through.
3 Drop the other foot flat down (da). Now try it with the other foot.

This whole movement resembles running on the spot. The best you can hope for at first is a scrape back. The scrape is quite acceptable for a while. Get the feel of making a noise as you pull that foot back. As you keep trying, the scrape will become shorter and shorter until you are able to get a sharp 'tap'. This will only come with practice, but it *will* come. You will get a great feeling when it happens. The hotch is used fairly regularly in tap dancing so make sure you can do it. Don't lose heart!

Once you feel fairly confident, dispense with the chair-back or whatever and try it free-standing.

Another way to do the hotch (ca) is to land on the same foot. You will find it best to land on the 'toe'. This will then be ca-toe whilst staying on one leg. You can then add a further beat by simply dropping the heel of the same foot: Ca-toe-he(R) or (L) – three beats.

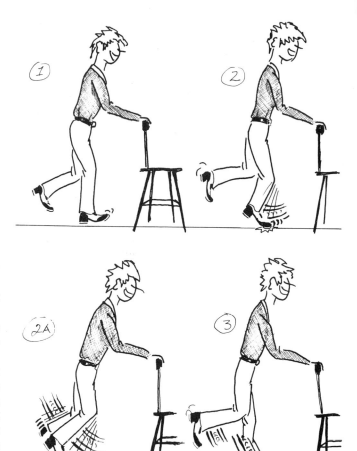

Fig 35 **Practising the hotch**

Time Hotch Step

The hotch can be an exciting new addition to the time step. After the first pu'pl, instead of the hop, make it a 'hotch-toe' (the hotch being written as 'ca' and indicated on the grid with an asterisk). The remainder of the time-step movement does not change. As usual, plenty of work is necessary to make the ca a clean, sharp beat but the added tap brings a new dimension to the step. I must point out that it is not *always* necessary to use the hotch in the time step. Many times the simple, basic step is best. The hotch is added when that little extra beat will give the routine another boost and keep your audience on the edge of their seats.

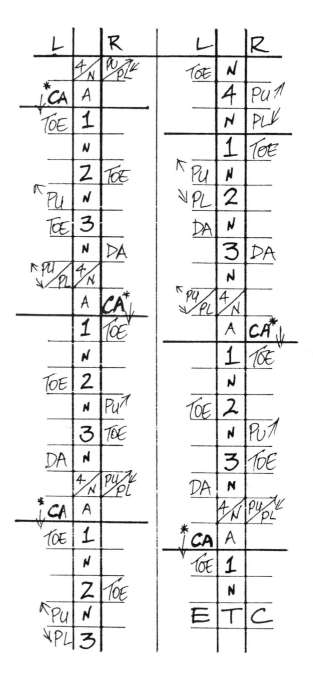

Fig 35a **Time hotch step; the hotch (ca) is marked with asterisks**

Da-pupple-ca

Now we use the hotch together with the pu'pl. As the foot is suspended behind, after the catchback, it snatches a pu'pl as follows:

1 Da(L) – this is the main beat and happens ON the beat.
2 Pu'pl(R) – as the R foot is suspended behind, it snatches a quick pu'pl at about the 4 o'clock position on the 'floor-clock' (see page 15).
3 The L foot is still in the da position and has to perform the ca as in hotch.
4 Now both feet are off the ground, you land on the R which is also the da as in 1 but on the other foot.
5 The L foot, now suspended behind, is ready to snatch a pu'pl at the 8 o'clock position.
6 Ca(R) (hotch).
7 Land on L returning to the da position as in 1. The da lands on each main beat of the bar ie 1, 2, 3, 4, with a pu'pl-ca between each count.

This step will take quite a bit of practice before you can get it working sweetly with nice even beats, but, when you *do* get it, you have mastered one of the fastest steps in tap dancing.

As this step *is* so quick, we have to accommodate it on the grid by splitting the squares. The counting has also to be slightly augmented. Up to this point, we have counted '1-n-2-n-3-n-4-n'. Or '1-n a 2 n a 3-n-a-4-n-a'. Now we have to introduce a new count for this quicker step. The best way to think of it is 'one a penny two a penny' etc, written on the grid like this:

'1-a-p-n-2-a-p-n-3-a-p-n-4-a-p-n'. (*see the split squares in Fig 37.*)

Notice the 1 is in the top half of the split square to correspond with the da(L). The 'a' is in the bottom half of the same square to correspond with the pu(R). The 'p' comes next and corresponds with the pl(R). Beneath the 'p' is the 'n' to correspond with the ca(L). So, the count of 1-a-p-n is da-pu'pl-ca. It all becomes quite clear after a while!

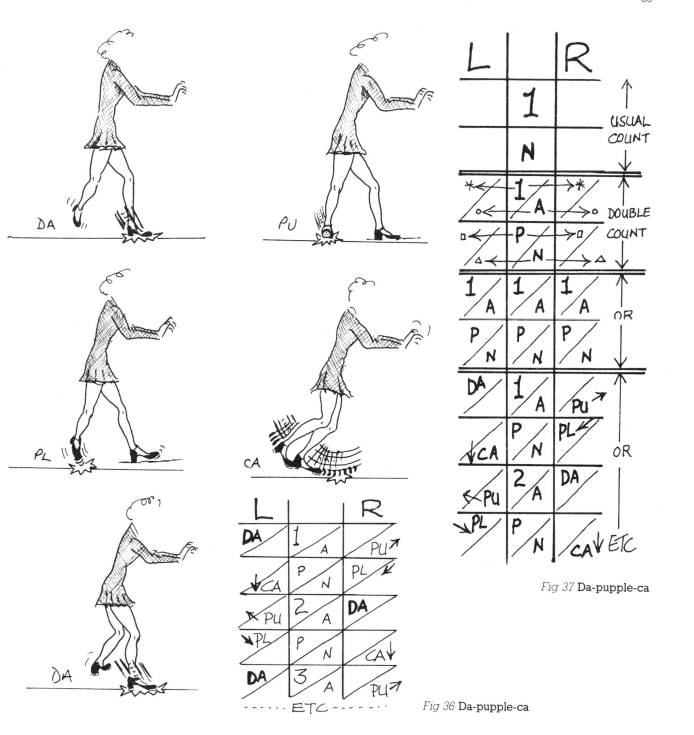

DA

PU

PL

CA

DA

L	R
	1
	N

← 1 →
o← A →o
□← P →□
△← N →△

USUAL COUNT

DOUBLE COUNT

L		R
1	1	1
A	A	A
P	P	P
N	N	N

OR

L		R
DA	1	PU ↗
	A	PL ↙
↓CA	P	
	N	
←PU	2	DA
	A	
↓PL	P	CA↓ ETC
	N	

OR

Fig 37 **Da-pupple-ca**

L		R
DA	1	PU ↗
	A	PL ↙
↓CA	P	
	N	**DA**
↖PU	2	
	A	CA↓
↓PL	P	
DA	N	PU ↗
	3	
	A	

- - - - - - ETC - - - - - -

Fig 36 **Da-pupple-ca**

Brush-plus

Having touched on the brush step (page 21), we can now work on it a little more. Have another look at it and we can take it from there.

1 Brush(R)
2 Hop(L)
3/4 Ca-toe(R)

Now:

5 Hop(R) (land on toe). (L foot swings forwards at 11 o'clock in preparation for the catchback.)
6 Ca(L) (swing L foot back catching toe on way through).
7 Hop(R) (L foot remains suspended behind).
8 Tip(L) (tip of L toe stabs floor behind and is raised again).
9 Hop(R).
10/11 Pu-toe(L) (left foot swings forwards in the direction of 11 o'clock, catches floor on way through and toe is put down, keeping heel raised).
12 Da(R) (flat foot is put down just a little way towards the L foot).
13 Da(L) (flat foot put down just a little way further towards 11 o'clock).

The whole of this section is counted like this:

1	-	2	an	3	-	4	an
Brush		hop	ca	toe		hop	ca
R		L	R	R		R	L

1	an	2	an	3	an	4
hop	tip	hop	pu	toe	da	da
R	L	R	L	L	R	L

The arms make this step look very classy and must be performed with plenty of showmanship. We are already familiar with the brush-hop-ca-toe where the arms are pushed up together in front of the face, then part to move outwards and round like a fountain, returning to the sides by 'toe'. Now, as you hop on the R foot (5) and the L foot swings forwards (11 o'clock), both arms swing to the left. They then begin to swing to the right so that they

are fully swung to the right by the time you are doing the tip(L) (8). On the pu-toe(L) da(R) da(L), they swing left again. They are then quickly returned to the belt-buckle position to start the 'fountain' again.

This step lasts for two bars of four-beat rhythm and can be repeated as often as you wish. If you start with the brush on the R foot, you stay on the R foot for each repeated sequence. Vice versa on the L.

There is a little more to add to the step once you have mastered it, rather like adding the break to the time steps. The brush sequence is danced three times, ending da(R) da(L). Now we add:

14 Ca(R)
15 Hop(L) (overleaf)
16 Tip(R)
17 Hop(L)
18/19 Pu-toe(R)
20 Da(L)
21 Da(R)
22 Ca(L)
23 Hop(R)
24 Tip(L)
25 Hop(R)
26/27 Pu-toe (L)
28 Da(R)
29 Da(L)

That's it! Now for the arms. As you dance 11 and 12, the arms are swinging to the left. (This being the third time, take 13a instead of 13 – see *Fig 38a*.) Through 13a and 14, keep the swing going left up and round full circle (together) so that by the 'tip' at 16 they are pointing left again. Swing back retracing the move out to the right, up and round, completing the circle pointing right as you 'tip' at 24. Finally swing half-way back to finish up with both pointing left for the finish at 29 (*see Fig 38b*).

Fig 38a **Brush-plus with arms**

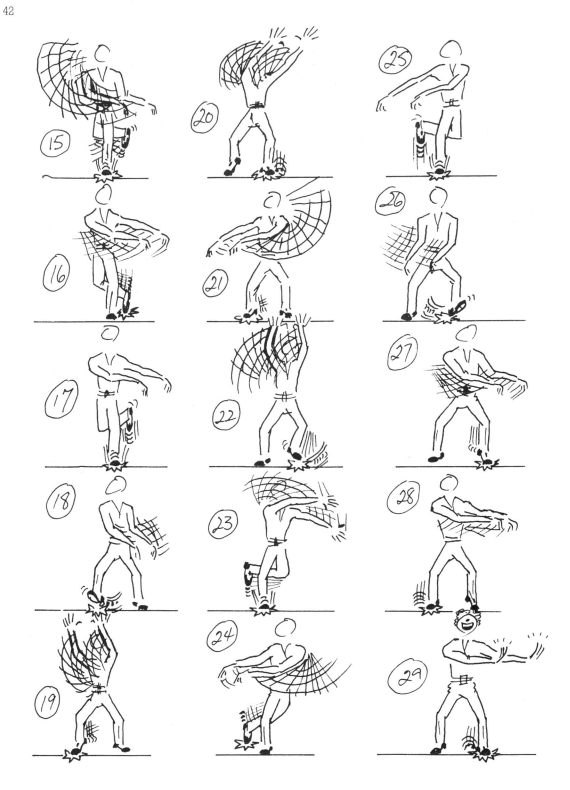

Fig 39 **Brush-plus**

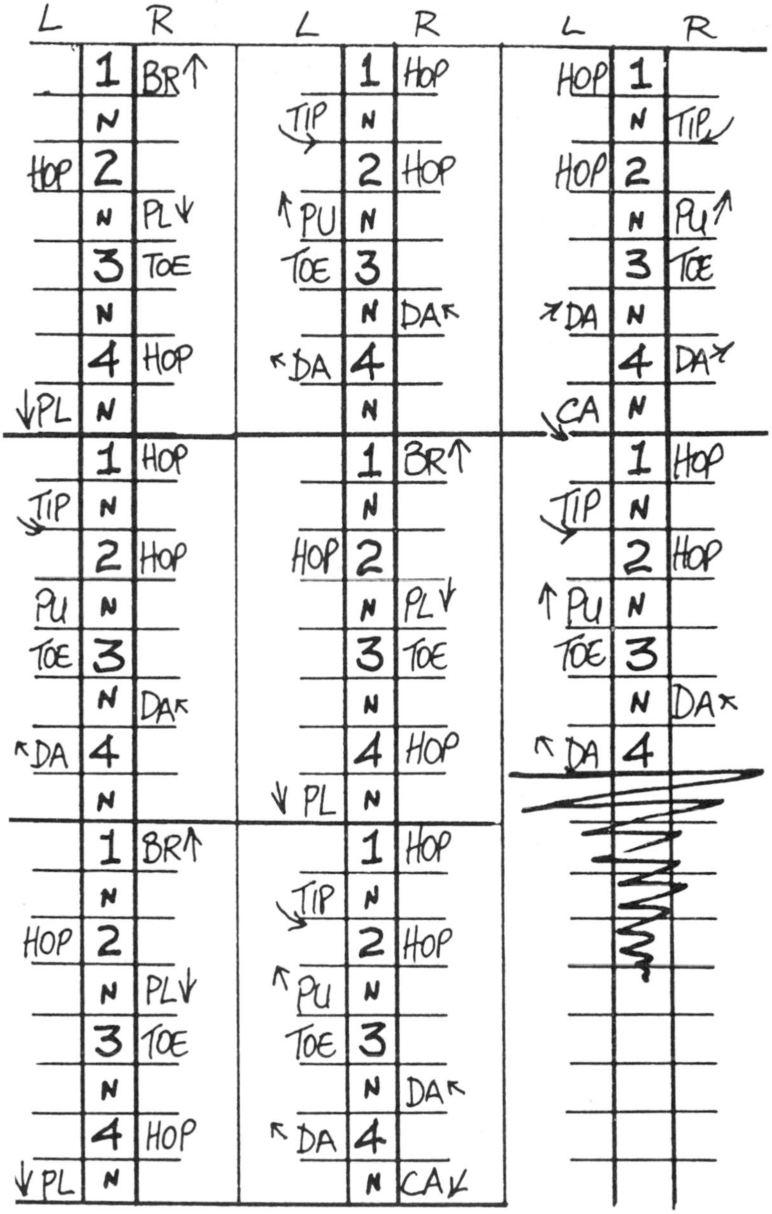

Top section

L	#	R		L	#	R		L	#	R
	1	BR↑			1	HOP		HOP	1	
	N			TIP→	N				N	TIP↘
HOP	2				2	HOP		HOP	2	
	N	PL↓		↑PU	N				N	PU↗
	3	TOE		TOE	3				3	TOE
	N				N	DA↖		↗DA	N	
	4	HOP		↖DA	4				4	DA↘
↓PL	N				N			↙CA	N	

Middle section

L	#	R		L	#	R		L	#	R
	1	HOP			1	BR↑			1	HOP
TIP↘	N				N			TIP↘	N	
	2	HOP		HOP	2				2	HOP
PU	N				N	PL↓		↑PU	N	
TOE	3				3	TOE		TOE	3	
	N	DA↖			N				N	DA↘
↖DA	4				4	HOP		↖DA	4	
	N			↓PL	N					

Bottom section

L	#	R		L	#	R
	1	BR↑			1	HOP
	N			TIP↘	N	
HOP	2				2	HOP
	N	PL↓		↑PU	N	
	3	TOE		TOE	3	
	N				N	DA↖
	4	HOP		↖DA	4	
↓PL	N				N	CA↙

Fig 38b **Brush-plus with arms (cont)**

Shunt

This is a very simple move. You step forwards on to your toe, then hop forwards another half or quarter pace and land on flat foot. The back leg is raised slightly as the front foot lands after the hop. If you are shunting on to the R foot, push your right arm out towards the 2 o'clock area and throw your left arm back in line with your L leg. These are approximate arm positions which can be altered according to how you or your teacher think it looks. The head position can also be adapted to your liking. The straight-ahead look is best in my opinion, but there are times when it will be effective to look down at the shunting foot. Remember not to flop if you do look down, keep the back straight and look down with pride!

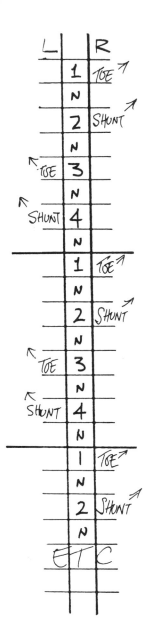

Fig 39a **Shunt**

(*above & opposite*) The shunt. Step out then shunt further out landing on flat foot

Turns

Fig 40a **Take-off position.** Arms raised around shoulder height, right arm, 3 o'clock, left arm, 9 o'clock. R foot prepared to push body in an anticlockwise direction. Eyes fixed on an object at head height.

Fig 40b L heel raised, R foot pushes body round. Arms swing in to chest adding impetus to the move. (The right arm is more important when turning anticlockwise, ie to the left.)

Fig 40c **Body turns.** The head stays perfectly still, keeping the eyes fixed on the object.

Fig 40d **Body further round.** The eyes stay fixed on the object as long as possible.

Fig 40e Just before the neck breaks! Swing the head round quickly.

Fig 40f **Look for the object again.** Remember, the head is last to leave and first to arrive. The body should be three-quarters of the way round by now.

Fig 40g **The eyes have found the object.** The body has completed a whole turn. The R foot is grounded, tapping the floor as well as putting the brakes on the turn. The arms are raised to the original position giving style to the move, at the same time being prepared to perform another turn if the routine requires it.

Sooner or later, you will have to tackle the turn. If you have never 'turned' before, here are a few basic principles. First of all, balance is all-important. Should you start into a turn whilst you are off-balance, you stand no chance of making a decent one and will very likely stagger around, losing control of the sequence.

Imagine a piece of string reaching from the top of your head to the ceiling. Keep your head at the centre of balance all the time. If you start a spinning-top going when it is off-balance, it will just fall down and spin out of control. So will you!

Spotting is also one of the keys to a nice, clean turn. By 'spotting', I mean picking out an object at about head height and fixing your eyes on it for 90 per cent of the turn. The body turns, but the eyes stay fixed on that object until your neck would break, then you quickly spin the head round and find your object again. If you are dancing in front of a mirror, then look at yourself. Your head should be last to leave and first to arrive. When you watch ballet dancers turning, you get the perfect example of how to 'spot'. Video, slow motion and stop frame techniques, are a great help when learning to turn, if you have access to them.

Do not be too eager to turn quickly straight away.

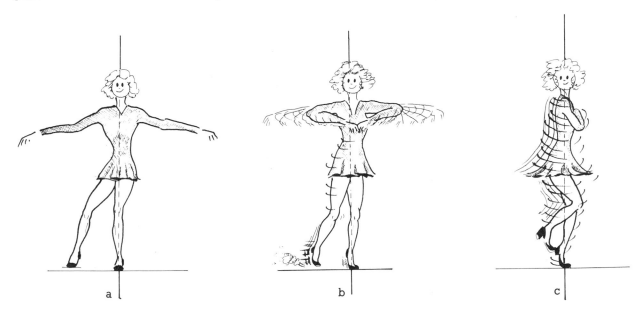

a   b   c

Start slowly, develop your confidence and gradually quicken up. Some of the most effective turns are slow ones.

Should you wear spectacles, it is wise either to take them off for the faster turns, or devise a way of keeping them on. Elastic around the back of your head, tied to each wing of the spectacles works quite well.

Your first turn must be *very* slow and done in stages. Stand straight, then, taking your main weight on your L foot, place your R foot out to the side at 3 o'clock. The R foot takes about a quarter of the weight. Raise your arms to about shoulder height, right arm 3 o'clock, left arm 9 o'clock. Now, three things happen at the same time. (I suggest you read to the end of this section before trying out a turn.)

1 Raise L heel so that the point of balance is centred on the ball of your L foot.
2 Push off with your R foot to give you the drive.
3 Swing the arms, from the elbows mainly, into your chest. This helps to give impetus along with the R foot push-off.

Once you get the idea and feel, you will be able to turn all the way round with one push-off, but the best way to start is using short steps. Starting with the R foot out at 3 o'clock, move to 2 o'clock, then 1 o'clock etc. At this stage, the arm movements are not necessary. You are simply getting used to 'spotting' and turning your head at the correct moment. You will quickly be able to skip alternate 'o'clock' positions, then progress to quarter turns, half turns and finally TARRA!

The turn described above is called a 'left outward' turn. Your L foot is grounded as the point of balance and you are turning to your left.

When you turn to your right, keeping the L foot grounded as the point of balance, you push off backwards with your R foot and swing your arms in, using the impetus of your left arm to pull you round. The spotting is the same technique, the other way round. As you push off with your R foot, it is tucked up in front of the left knee for the journey round and ready to be put down on 'arrival'. This is called a 'right inward' turn. You are turning right with your L foot as point of balance. The 'right outward' turn is when you turn to the right with the R foot grounded as the point of balance.

The 'left inward' turn is when you turn to your left whilst your R foot is grounded. Looking down from a bird's eye view, a left turn is anticlockwise, the right turn is clockwise.

d   e   f   g

You can see what the left outward turn looks like on the grid (*Fig 41a*).

Notice for this particular step, the turn starts on the first beat of the second bar. It is written in the L foot column, meaning that the L foot is the grounded one. The curve bends outwards to the left or anticlockwise. This is the left outward turn. The curved line starts on the first beat and continues through to the third beat. This is the time value of the turn. A turn could last any number of beats according to where the curved line starts and finishes.

When the L foot is grounded, but you are required to turn clockwise (to the right); the curve will be shown as in *Fig 41b*. The weight is still on the L foot and is shown in the L foot column, but the turn is to the right. (*For right outward and left*

inward turns, see Fig 41c.)

Practise these turns all four ways, L out and in, R out and in.

I must stress the importance of taking the turns carefully until you can perform them with ease and a pleasant look on your face. If it looks painful to you, your audience will be made to feel uneasy, so the more you practise, the more confident you will become and your audience will be more relaxed and receptive.

A simple summary of the turns is:

	turning anticlockwise	turning clockwise
Left outward	left foot grounded	—
Left inward	right foot grounded	—
Right outward	—	right foot grounded
Right inward	—	left foot grounded

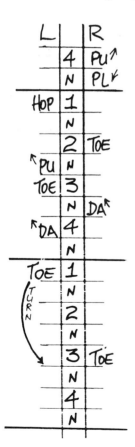

Fig 41a Left outward turn

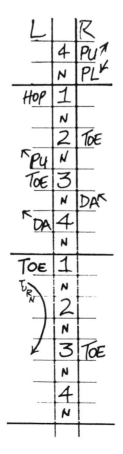

Fig 41b Right inward turn

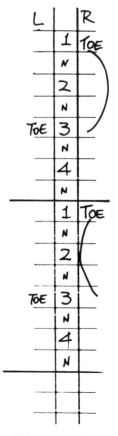

Fig 41c Right outward turn in first bar (above) followed by left inward turn

Preparation, looking at something straight

Quarter turn, eyes on same spot

Half turn, eyes still on same spot

Three-quarter turn, head spins round quickly and eyes find spot again

Turn completed

Repeats

Now that we are getting quite a few steps together, our grid is going to get longer and longer. When a step or sequence is repeated, it is both laborious and time-consuming to write it out twice. There is a simple way of indicating repeats on the grid.

The example in *Fig 42a* portrays the way a repeated bar appears. 'A' is just an ordinary four-beat bar and anything written in it is just danced once. 'B' is cornered off with a double line at the start and finish of the required repeated step or sequence. This can be any number of bars according to the length of the sequence to be repeated. In this case, you would have to dance whatever was written within the repeat signs four times, then continue with the routine from bar 'C' onwards.

Fig 42b is an example of dancing the single time-step break four times, then continuing.

Fig 42c shows the brush-plus routine we learned earlier. It was almost possible to repeat the first two bars 3 times except for the ca (asterisked) in the 4-n bar the third time through.

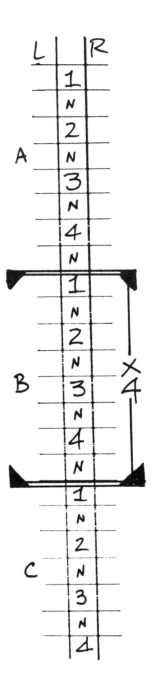

Fig 42a **Repeated bars**

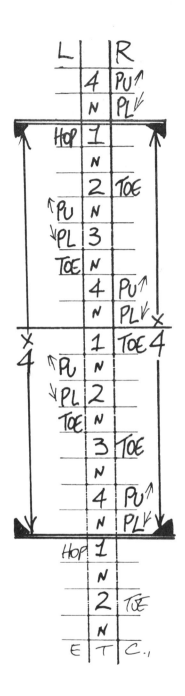

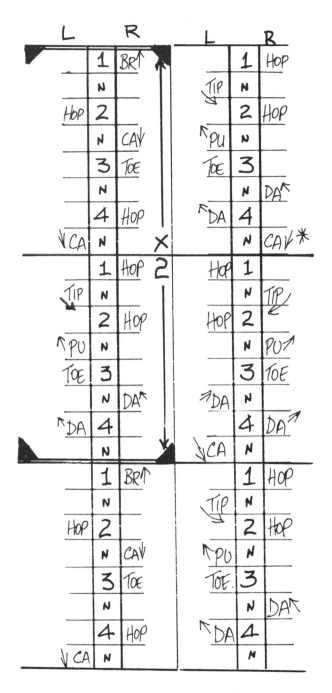

Fig 42b **Single time-step break repeated four times**

Fig 42c **Brush-plus with repeated bars**

Alpha-beat Routine

This is a thirty-two bar chorus in four-beat rhythm which incorporates some of the new steps and grid techniques.

Starting at the top of column 1, we have two bars of intro music to set the tempo. The dancing starts at letter A which we shall also call bar 1. The bars are numbered and ringed for easy reference.

Column 1, bar 1, square 1: R toe steps towards 2 o'clock.

Col 1, bar 1, sq 2: R foot shunts further towards 2 o'clock. The rest of bar 1 and bar 2 is fairly obvious.

Col 2, bars 3 and 4: the first two bars are repeated on the opposite feet.

These first four bars are then repeated, making 8 bars in all.

Col 3, bars 5 and 6: move backwards slightly. The arms are opposite to the feet, as the L foot pu'pls, the R arm is forward, L arm back and vice-versa.

Col 3, bar 7: as toes are put down, turn to the right until facing front again for the 'da' (bar 8, sq 1). The hand claps are above the head.

Col 4, bars 9, 10, 11 and 12: the previous step is repeated on opposite feet. The end of bar 12 starts us into the single time-step with break (bars 13, 14, 15 and 16).

Col 7, bars 17, 18, 19, and 20: triple time-step with break.

Col 8, bar 21: the brush-plus step is used here apart from the last part (bar 26, sq 3). The step ends earlier to make the repeat of the whole sequence a little easier. The routine can be repeated as often as you wish by returning to letter 'A' (bar 1).

Good tunes for this routine would be *Bring me Sunshine, Bye-bye Blues, Bye-bye Blackbird, Mack the Knife* and *Cute*, or any of the tunes suggested for the final three routines (pages 106–143).

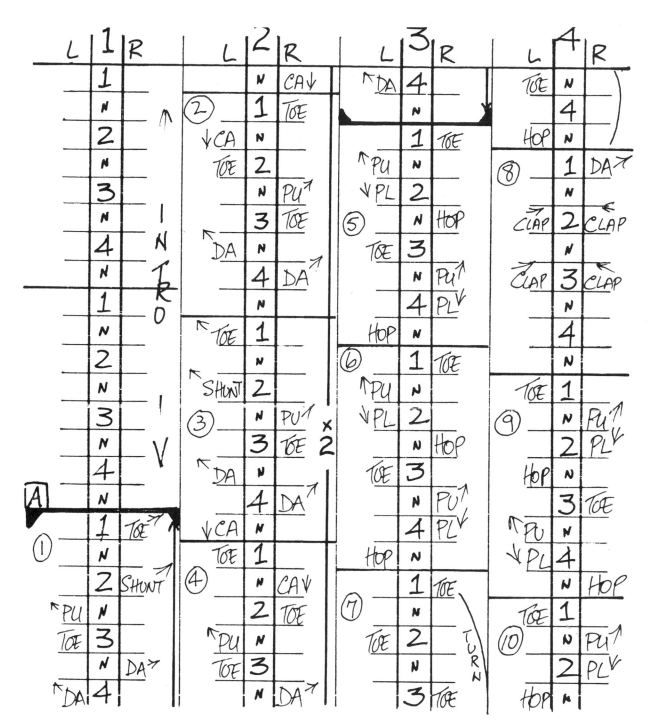

Fig 42d **Alpha-beat routine** *(beginning)*

54

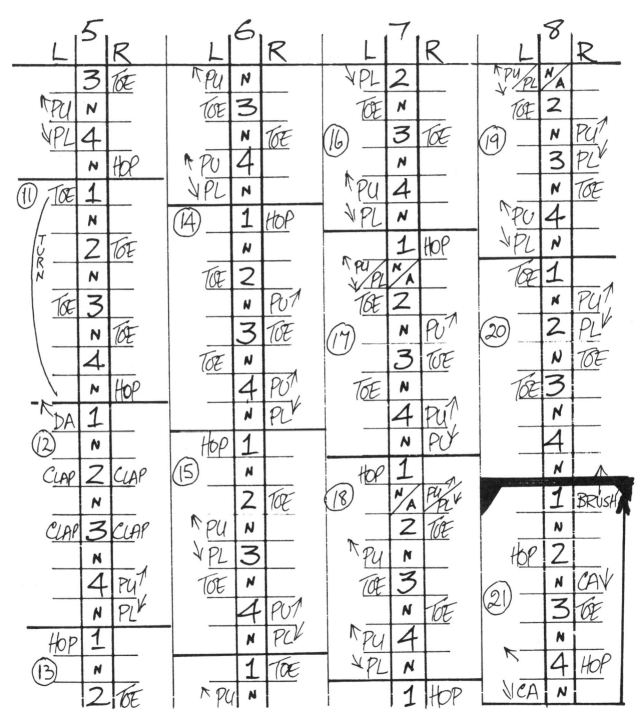

Fig 42e **Alpha-beat routine** *(cont)*

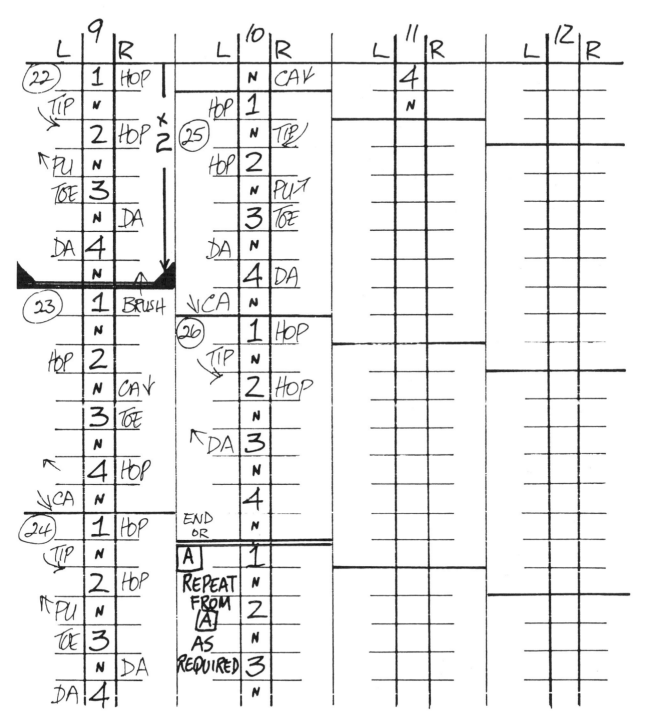

Fig 42f **Alpha-beat routine** *(end)*

Tapioca

This is an exercise in close beating as we make extra special use of the 'dig'. The 'tapioca' step is an ankle-loosener and there is very little movement involved. It is designed to notch up lots of beats whilst apparently standing still. It is also helpful in establishing a closer relationship between brain, toe and heel.

The word 'tapioca' is merely an identifying nickname for the movement. The actual step in tap terms is dig-ca-toe-heel, all with the same foot (*Fig 43*). On the fourth beat (heel) the other heel is raised in readiness to start the dig-ca-toe-heel without a break in the rhythm. The beats should be exactly even. Do not substitute speed for accuracy! Practise until you can get a continuous flow of beats without an obvious hiccup in the rhythm as you change feet.

When you are satisfied that you are in control of tapioca, we add a little extra and do the 'double-double-yolker'. After the first dig-ca, instead of following it with the toe-he, repeat the dig-ca and *then* the toe-he – six beats. Like this:
Dig-ca-dig-ca-toe-he(R) (double-double-yolker)
Dig-ca-dig-ca-toe-he(L).

Practise this until it is as comfortable as tapioca, then we can put them together like this:

1 Da(L)
2 Double-double-yolker(R)
3 Tapioca(L)
4 Da(R)
5 Pause (one beat)
6 Da(R)
7 Double-double-yolker(L)
8 Tapioca(R)
9 Da-da-da(L)
10 Double-double-yolker(R)
11 Double-double-yolker(L)
12 Tapioca(R)
13 Tapioca(L)
14 Double-double-yolker(R)
15 Da(L)

The arms can hang loosely by your side or you can invent something for yourself. Have a look at it on the grid (*Fig 44*).

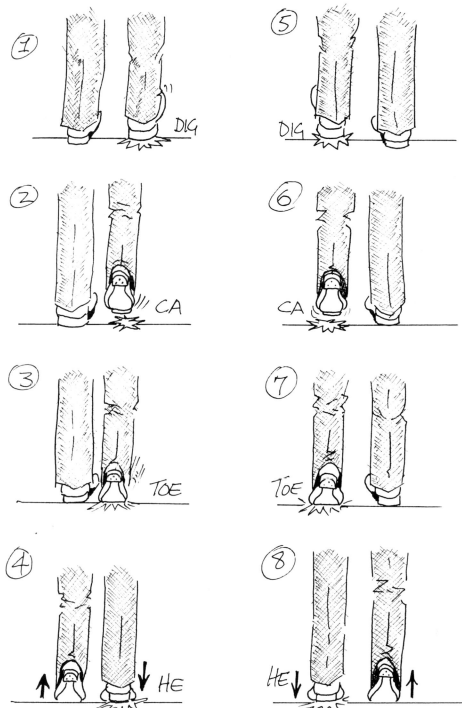

Fig 43 **Tapioca**

L		R		L		R		L		R
DA	1			HE	N				4	DIG
	N				1	DIG			N	CA↓
	2	DIG			N	CA↓			1	TOE
	N	CA↓			2	TOE			N	HE
	3	DIG			N	HE		DIG	2	
	N	CA↓		DA	3			↓CA	N	
	4	TOE			N			TOE	3	
	N	HE		DA	4			HE	N	
DIG	1				N				4	DIG
↓CA	N			DA	1				N	CA↓
TOE	2				N				1	DIG
HE	N				2	DIG			N	CA↓
	3	DA			N	CA↓			2	TOE
	N				3	DIG			N	HE
	4				N	CA↓		DA	3	
	N				4	TOE				
	1	DA			N	HE				
	N			DIG	1					
DIG	2			↓CA	N					
↓CA	N			DIG	2					
DIG	3			↓CA	N					
↓CA	N			TOE	3					
TOE	4			HE	N					

Fig 44 Tapioca and double-double-yolker

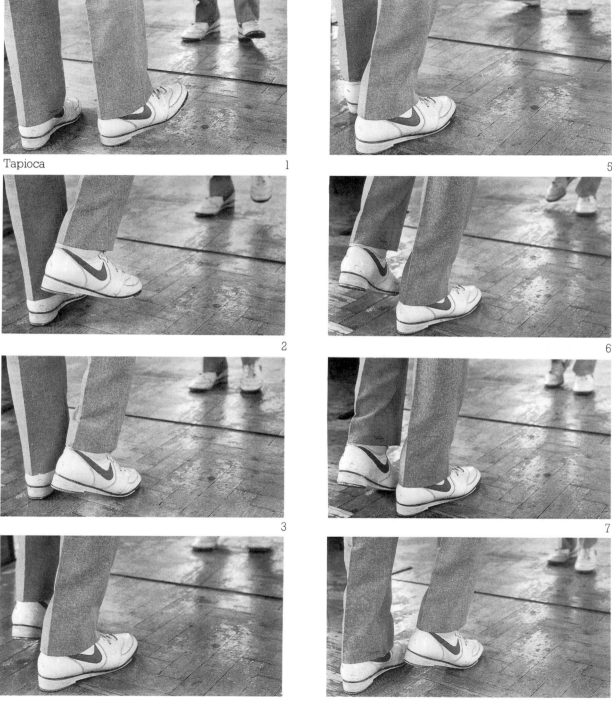

Tapioca

1

2

3

4

5

6

7

8

Heel-kick (Hik)

When one foot passes behind another, it is often possible to catch the heel of the front foot by the toe of the foot passing behind (*Fig 45a and b*). Try using the 'hik' in this sequence:

1 Ca-toe(R)
2 Ca-toe(L)
3 Pu'pl(R)
4 Hop(L)
5 Toe(R). Note: After the pu'pl of step 3 (during the hop of step 4), the R foot begins crossing the front of the hopping L foot and the toe is put down in front of, and to the left of, the left toe.
6 Hik(L). Here is the new step. As the L foot moves across the back of the R heel, the L toe catches the R heel and registers a beat. Do not worry if this beat is not as sharp as tapping the floor.
7 He(R). As soon as the R heel has been 'hikked', it is dropped on the spot.
8 Da(L). The L foot has now travelled past the back of the R foot, hikked it and is now put down, flat foot, and prepares for the same step using the other foot and travelling in the opposite direction.

When the pu'pl of step 3 is on the R foot, the step travels from right to left and vice versa. Have a look at it on the grid (*Fig 46*).

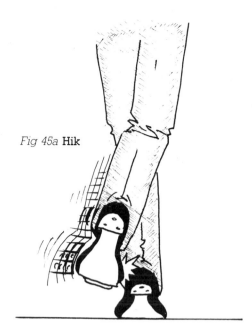

Fig 45a **Hik**

Fig 45b **Hik**

Fig 46 **Hik**

Cramp Roll

First of all we will look at the simple cramp roll, then we will add a few minor alternatives. This step is very compact and can be developed into an extremely fast, close-beat sequence.
The basic step is simply toe(R) toe(L) heel(R) heel(L). Slowly at first, then faster until you can jump into it and get four fast beats. Try also starting with the L foot so that you can perform it equally well with either foot. Whichever toe you start with, you must put the same heel down first. On the grid, the cramp roll is written 'CR' in each lane with a little cross indicating which toe should come first (*Fig 47A*).

We can now add a little to the beginning of the cramp roll, a pu. Before putting the first toe down, try a pu, making it pu-toe (*Fig 47B*). You now have:
1 Pu-toe(R)
2 Toe(L)
3 He(R)
4 He(L)

Also try starting with the L foot. Another addition at the start is ca(R) he(L), continuing with pu'toe-toe-he-he (*Fig 48C*). We now have:
1 Ca(R)
2 He(L)
3 Pu-toe(R)
4 Toe(L)
5 He(R)
6 He(L)

This sequence fits well with a three-beat rhythm. The three main beats are on the 'he' of square 1, the 'toe' of square 2, and the 'he' of square 3:

ca	HE	-	pu	TOE	toe	he	HE!
a	ONE [(an)]	a	a	TWO	an	a	THREE!

Practise this with alternate feet so that you can keep a steady three-beat rhythm going.
A tiny alteration can make a difference to the feel of the same rhythm. Instead of the last 'heel' of each sequence, make it a DA. Slam the flat foot down making it the strongest beat of the step. So, for this interpretation, change the 'he' on the third-beat to da. It is still quite simple to follow it with the ca, starting the step on the other foot (*Fig 48D*). The fastest version of this step is to change the third-beat step yet again (*Fig 48E*). This time, make it a dig! This does not need emphasis because we are going for speed. The position of the dig leaves the toe suspended, ready for the immediate ca to start the step again on the other foot. With practice, this version of the step can be very fast indeed. Again, it is best to work slowly at first. Make sure you are tapping all the beats properly before you even consider quickening. Do not forfeit clarity for speed.
You now have a few different versions of the cramp roll, it is up to you to make it a successful part of your repertoire.

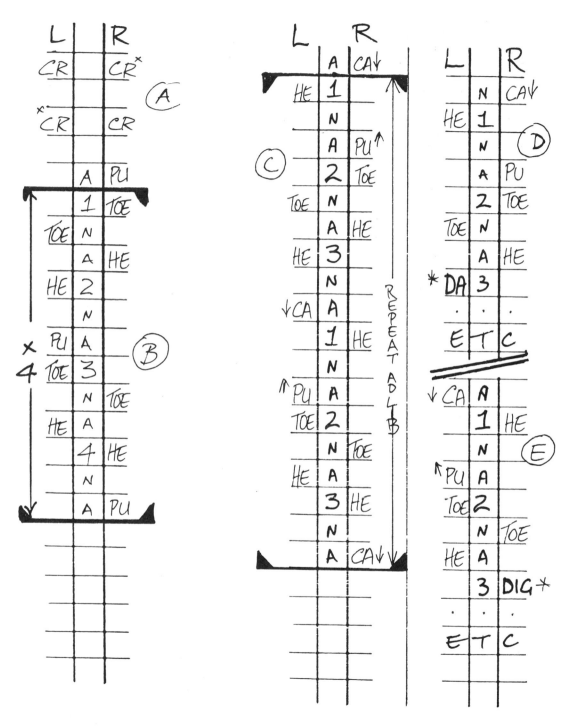

Fig 47 **Basic cramp roll**   Fig 48 **Cramp roll variations**

Flam

The flam consists of three beats almost together. A hop on the L foot immediately followed by a pu-toe on the R foot, the main stress being on the 'toe' which lands *on* the beat. The preceding hop-pu is fractionally before it and is not really worth putting in the half-beat square preceding the toe. The best way to portray the flam on the grid is as shown in *Fig 49A*.

The hop is shown in the L foot column on the same beat as the pu-toe in the R foot column. The word 'flam' is just a way of giving the step instant recognition. Naturally, when the flam is performed on the L foot, it is written as in *Fig 49B*. *Fig 49C* shows a way in which the flam can be used. As you brush(L) on beat 3-n of the second bar, it is good to hop(R) at the same time and land on beat 1 of the next bar as you flam(L).

This flam step can be repeated using alternate feet for as long as you like. Each sequence measures two bars of four-beat music, so once on each foot is a four-bar measure and fits well into many routines.

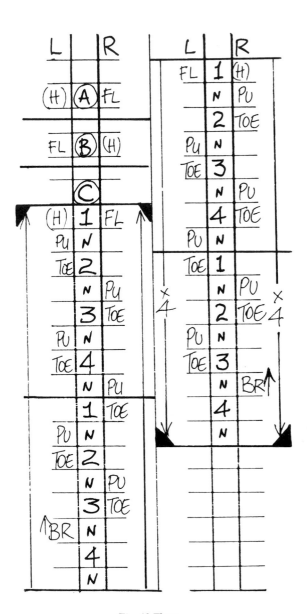

Fig 49 **Flam**

Trenches (R)

Trenches

The trenches are the good old-fashioned applause-getters. Many an ordinary routine can be whipped up into a show-biz frenzy by finishing with the trenches.

It is merely a running-on-the-spot step but made to look semi-acrobatic by leaning forward and sliding the feet back with each step. Swinging opposite arms to legs and keeping the hands nice and low completes the picture (*Fig 50*). Normally you would change feet for every beat of the bar, giving you four trenches (two on each foot) to each four-beat bar.

The trench is written as 'TR' in the lane of the foot which is landing up front. The arrow in the corresponding square in the other lane represents the slide-back of the other foot.

Fig 51 is a short routine incorporating the trench step with hops, tips and a showy turn as explained overleaf. This is a fairly athletic step but a good finish to any routine.

Trenches changeover

Fig 50 **Trenches**

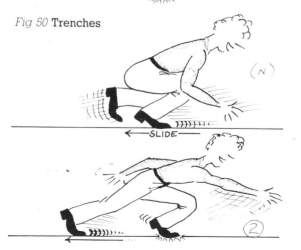

Trenches (L)

Reading the grid along with the illustrations in *Fig 52*, this step is not easy to explain, but looks very good when performed well. The four trenches are simple enough, but the following steps are performed during a turn which has to look like an aeroplane's propeller from the audience's point of view.

Bar 1

Beat 1 diag 1 tr(R)
Beat 2 diag 2 tr(L)
Beat 3 diag 3 tr(R)
Beat 4 diag 4 tr(L)
Beat 4-n diag 5 tip(R). R foot is in position behind and easily gets an on-the-spot tip. Arms move out sideways, ready to start the propeller movement. Throughout the next few steps, the arms are fully extended and swing round, right arm travels upwards, left arm downwards. The body swivels during the turn and the head tries to stay in a position that would be occupied by the nose of the propeller.

Bar 2

Beat 1 diag 6 hop(L). Arms begin to swing as body begins to swivel.
Beat 1-n diag 7 toe(R). Turn and swivel continues.
Beat 2 diag 8 tip(L). Body is now half-way through turn, back is to audience, body swivel should be in a lean-back position with top of head (propeller nose) 'facing' the audience.
Beat 2-n diag 9 hop(R). Body now three-quarters of the way through the turn with the arms almost having completed a full circle.
Beat 3 diag 10 da(L). Turn completed, arms coming out of propeller position.
Beat 3-n. No tap beat here, prepare for final step.
Beat 4 diag 11 da(R). This step can be either the end of sequence or end of routine in which case the L foot remains grounded and the da(R) completes the *tarra!* attitude which means 'applause now please'! However, should you wish to repeat the step using the opposite feet, the da(R) becomes more of a hop (diag 12) as the L foot is raised ready for the tr(L) which starts the whole sequence going the other way. I advise you to give this step lots of practice in both directions. The selling point of the sequence is, of course, the swinging arms and swivelling trunk in order to give the propeller effect. Don't forget to perfect this step so well that you can also smile!

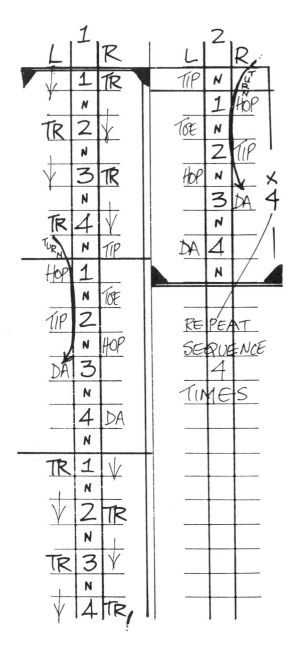

Fig 51 **Routine with trenches**

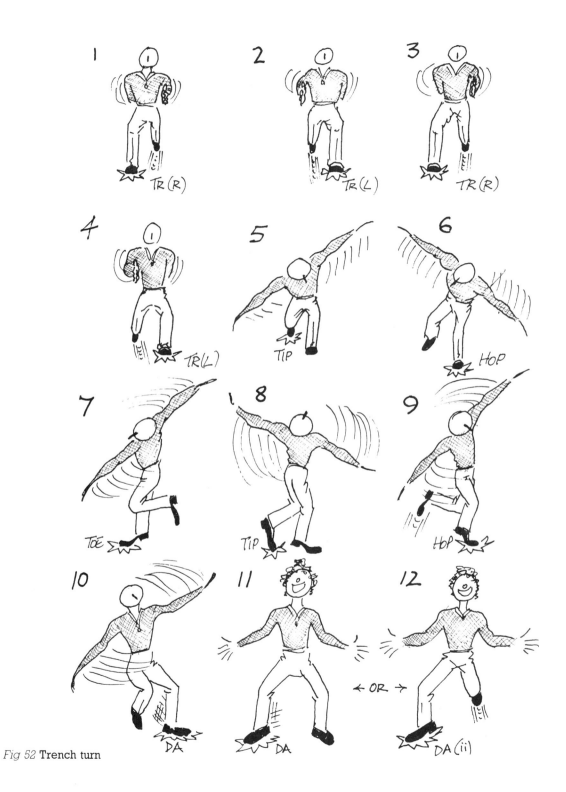

Fig 52 **Trench turn**

Pu-he-pl

This is one of my favourite beats when moving into the 'close-beat' style of tapping. The normal pu'pl can be made into three beats by making use of the heel in between the pu and pl. As the toe taps the forward movement of the pu, the heel (he) touches the floor before the toe returns for the pl. The heel does not travel forward after it has touched the floor, but stops at the 'dig' position. The movement is very tight and the three beats are quick. Instead of just having pu'pl, you have pu-he-pl in the same space of time. A good way to get used to this addition is to practise the pu-he-pl followed by putting the working foot flat down(da):

Pu-he-pl-da(R), Pu-he-pl-da(L). (*See Fig 53*)

Now try the pu-he-pl followed by putting the toe down, leaving the heel suspended. Practise with both feet equally or if one foot is a little more sluggish than the other, give it extra treatment.

Another addition to this sequence is the heel of the other foot between the pl and 'toe' of the working foot. This works out as follows:

Pu-he-pl(R) he(L) toe(R).

The counting for this addition is: one a penny two. Then with the opposite feet:

Pu-he-pl(L) he(R) toe(L).

The counting for the two together is: one a penny two, three a penny four, one a penny two, three a penny four, and so on. Look at it on the grid (*Fig 54*).

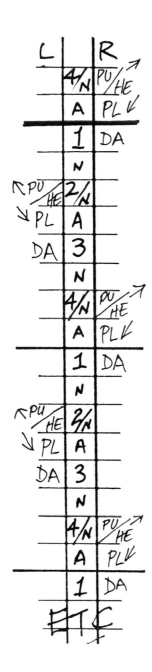

Fig 53 **Pu-he-pl-da**

Fig 54 **Pu-he-pl-he-toe**

Pu-he-pl Time-step

Once you have perfected the pu-he-pl, it can be introduced into many of the steps already mastered. The first one to spring to mind is the time step. The very first pu'pl can be altered to a pu-he-pl, whereby three beats are tapped instead of the normal two. This works very well for the single (*Fig 55*) and double time-step (*Fig 56*). When performing the triple time-step, only use the pu-he-pl instead of the 'first' pu'pl and leave the 'second' pu'pl (after the hop) as normal. It is possible to make this second pu'pl into a pu-he-pl but it is a bit messy and tends to sound scrambled. By all means try it and see, but I think you will find it neater to keep that second pu'pl of the triple time-step unaltered. Have a look at it on the grid (*Fig 57*).

When you are ready for another challenge, try adding the hotch (ca) to the pu-he-pl time-step. It can be very good when it is sharp and clean, but can also sound muddy if not performed well. It is well worth the effort once all the beats are rattling out like a machine gun. As it is very fast, the grid becomes somewhat involved, but a little concentration should clarify the situation (*Fig 58*).

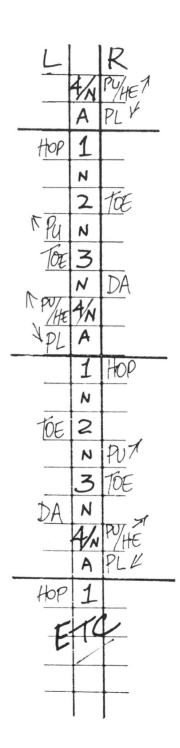

Fig 55 **Single time-step with pu-he-pl**

Fig 56 — Left diagram

	L	R
	4/N	PU/HE ↗
	A	PL ↙
HOP	1	
	N	PU ↑
	2	TOE
↑ PU	N	
TOE	3	
	N	DA
↑ PU/HE ↓ PL	4/N	
↓ PL	A	
	1	HOP
↖ PU	N	
TOE	2	
	N	PU ↗
	3	TOE
DA	N	
	4/N	PU/HE ↗
	A	PL ↓
HOP	1	

ETC

Fig 57 — Middle diagram

	L	R	
	4/N	PU/HE ↑	(HEEL)
	A	PL ↓	
HOP	1/N	PU ↑	(NO HEEL)
	A	PL ↓	
	2	TOE	
↑ PU	N		
TOE	3		
	N	DA	
(HEEL) ↑ PU/HE ↓ PL	4/N		
↓ PL	A		
(NO HEEL) ↑ PU ↓ PL	1/N	HOP	
↓ PL	A		
TOE	2		
	N	PU ↑	
	3	TOE	
DA	N		
	4/N	PU/HE ↑	(HEEL)
	A	PL ↓	
HOP	1/N	PU ↑	(NO HEEL)
	A	PL ↓	
	2	TOE	

E T C

Fig 58 — Right diagram

	L	R
	4/A	PU/HE ↗
↓ CA	P/N	PL ↙
TOE	1	
	N	
	2	TOE
↖ PU	N	
TOE	3	
	N	DA
↖ PU/HE ↓ PL	4/A	
↓ PL	P/N	CA ↓
	1	TOE
	N	

ETC

Fig 56 **Double time-step with pu-he-pl**   *Fig 57* **Triple time-step with pu-he-pl**   *Fig 58* **Pu-he-pl time-step with hotch**

Wing

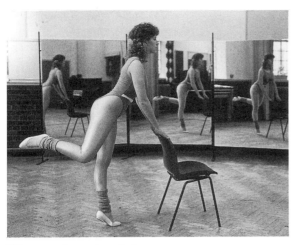

Wing practice using chair

The four stages of the wing: prepare to fling sideways, foot flung out to side, ca as foot catches on way back in, toe lands

The wing is one of the more advanced steps and it must be understood that this will take time to master. Once you can wing, you are really getting somewhere in the world of tap dancing. Again, this is a showy step and is well worth the effort. First we will look at what it entails, then we will tackle the methods of practice.

The 'single' wing is performed by one leg only. The unused foot is suspended just above ankle height. The working foot has to hop, *but* between hopping and landing the toe must be flicked outwards, scraping the floor, then flicked back inwards, catching the floor along the way – four different stages as shown in *Fig 59.*

1 Prepare to hop on the working foot whilst raising the non-working foot to just over ankle height. The working foot must be prepared to hop and flick out to the side.
2 The working foot hops and flicks out sideways, scraping the floor before becoming airborne.
3 The working foot is immediately pulled back inwards, catching the toe on the floor for one sharp beat before becoming airborne again.
4 The working foot lands on the ball of the foot and either prepares to repeat movement, or prepares for next step, or stops at end of routine.

The best way to get the feel of the wing is to practise the movement from a sitting position (*Fig 60*). Practise with each foot separately. Once you are confident of the wing sitting down, the next step is to try it whilst holding on to a chair-back or a similar support to take the body weight and keep you steady (*Fig 61*). Practise the wing with each foot separately until you are really 'in charge' and getting a good sharp tap with the middle beat (3) between the scrape and landing. (*For the grid, see Fig 63, A and B.*)

Once you are ready to try winging without holding on, the secret is to get as much height as possible with the hop. This will give you more time and room to perform the flick before landing. The arms can help. As the hop begins, fling the elbows up above shoulder height to help you get well off the ground. Try to avoid looking down at your feet and *smile!*

PUSH SIDEWAYS ①

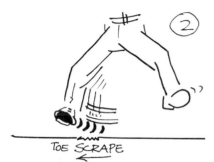

TOE SCRAPE ②

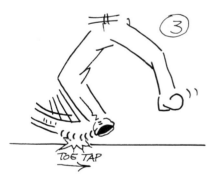

TOE TAP ③

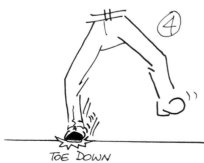

TOE DOWN ④

Fig 59 **Wing**

Fig 60 **Practising the wing (sitting)**

Fig 61 **Practising the wing (holding on to a support)**

Fig 62 **Wing with arm movements**

Double Wing

The double wing (*Fig 63C*) is simply a case of doing the single wing with both feet at the same time. Both feet travel outwards, away from each other, doing the scrape; then they travel inwards towards each other picking up the tap at the same time, then landing together. The beats should be exactly together so there are no extra taps to be gained. The only difference is in the appearance of the movement. The arms are still required to help with the upwards movement from the double hop.

When the double wing is mastered, it is possible to offset the step by winging with one foot fractionally later than the other, eg set R foot off on the scrape outwards, straightaway set the L foot off. Pull the R foot back, catching the floor for its tap, immediately followed by the L; land on the R foot closely followed by the L foot. Not counting the noise made by the scrape, you get the two taps from the R and L 'toes' as they pull inwards, then the two beats as they land separately – four beats without counting the scrape. The rhythm of the offset wing fits the word 'tiddley-pom'! The main beat normally is the final one (pom) – tiddley-ONE, tiddley-TWO, etc.

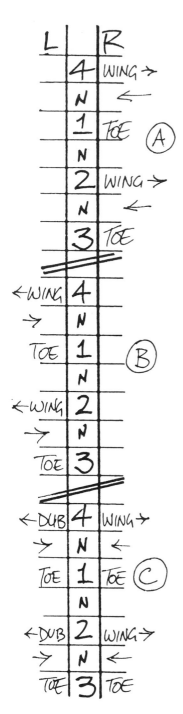

Fig 63 **A** Single wing(R), **B** single wing(L), and **C** double wing

Pendulum Wing

This time we have a single wing on one foot whilst the other foot swings forwards and back, catching the floor with the toe once for each swing. The swinging foot resembles a pendulum, hence the name given to the step. Whilst the pendulum foot swings back and forth, it is not put down and does not take any weight. The winging foot performs exactly as in the normal single wing.

If we are winging with the R foot, the R foot performs the whole wing, returning to the landing position before the L foot swings forwards, catching 'toe' on the floor, and continues swinging forwards. When the L foot is at about knee height, the R foot wings again and lands, then the L foot swings back, catching the floor again, and continues swinging backwards. (The knee can bend a little as the foot remains suspended behind, waiting to swing forwards again.)

That is all the pendulum wing consists of and it can be repeated as many times as you like. Practise equally with each foot and if one foot is more obstinate than the other, give it a little overtime!

The rhythm of this wing can be explained through the phrase, 'wing-an-a-tick, wing-an-a-tock, wing-an-a-tick, wing-an-a-tock. The word 'wing' being the scrape sideways, the 'an' being the tap as the foot is pulled back inwards, the 'a' being the toe down and the 'tick' being the swinging tap forwards by the other foot. The 'tock' is the swinging tap backwards. The main beat of this step is normally on the 'tick' and 'tock', ie wing-an-a-TICK, wing-an-a-TOCK, or, wing-an-a-ONE, wing-an-a-TWO etc.

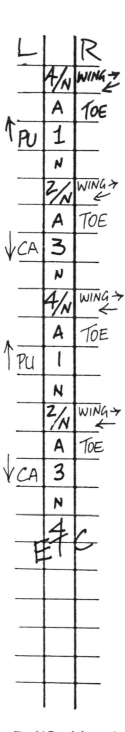

Fig 64 **Pendulum wing**

Side-klik

Here we have a sideways movement incorporating a jump and a click of the heels. This step can be large or small according to the requirements of the routine.

We will start with a R side klik (on the grid it will be written 'sk').

1 L foot steps across and in front of R foot, puts toe down; the heel remains suspended.
2 R foot swings out to the right without touching the floor.
3 L foot hops up towards the suspended R foot and the R foot moves a little towards the oncoming L foot and they click heels together.
4 L foot returns toe to floor taking the whole body weight whilst the R foot remains suspended. If you are feeling extra energetic, the R foot could travel slightly upwards again after the klik.

When performing the side-klik to the left, the R foot steps across and the whole procedure is transferred to the other side. The step bears repeating quite a few times, first to one side, then the other. When the side-klik is a small one, the hop need only be a few centimetres and it looks cute and cheeky. When it is big and energetic, it is almost balletic.

The arms are useful in getting the height for the big klik. Start to swing them upwards and sideways as the first foot takes the step across, keep them raised until the step is completed, then lower them in order to swing them up again as the step is repeated to the other side.

Figs 65 & 66 **Side-klik**

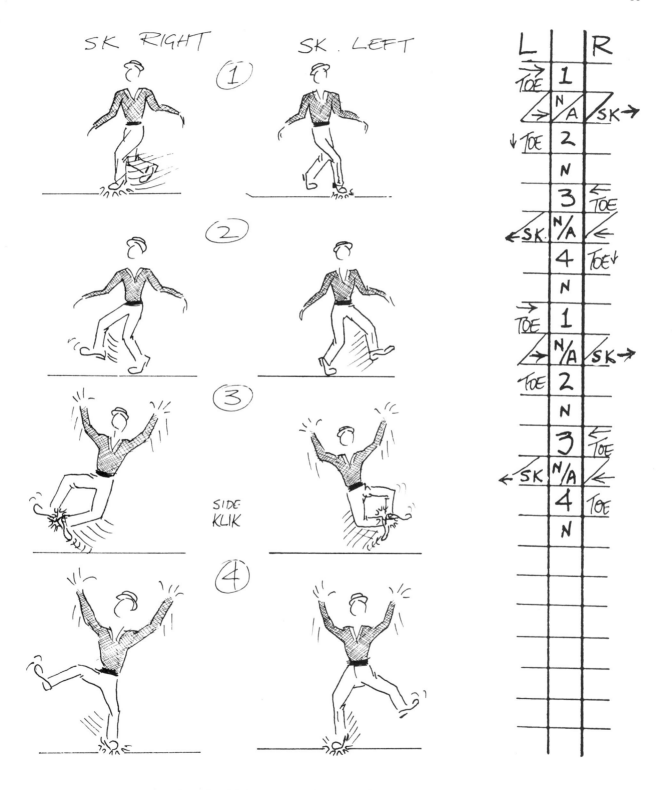

Slurp

Slurp performed forwards and back instead of sideways. L foot kicks forwards as L foot slurps forward and is joined by R foot as it is put down

R foot kicks backwards as R foot slurps backwards and is joined by L foot as it is put down

The slurp is a very light-hearted, comical step often used by clowns or sloppily clothed tramps making full use of overlarge boots.

One of the main points is transference of weight, knowing which way you are going next.

Let's try starting with a left slurp.

1 L foot swings out sideways keeping the knee bent and pointing out left. This movement pulls the body along to the left.

2 R foot follows but remains in contact with the floor and slides along.

3 L foot lands at exactly the same time as the R foot finishes its slide along the floor and they should end up side by side. From this position it is possible to either slurp again to the left or reverse the movement and slurp back to the right.

It is possible to keep slurping in one direction for as long as you like, whatever the routine demands. The thing to remember is weight transference. If you start with a left slurp, your weight must be taken by the R foot to allow the L foot to take off and also to push itself into the slide across. If you are going to continue with another left slurp, the weight must stay with the R foot. When you are going to change directions and slurp back to the right, weight must be transferred to the L foot to allow the R foot to take off. The traditional arm movement for the slurp is to imagine you are holding a short piece of string between your hands and swing them in a bent position, the same direction as the slurp (*Fig 67*). The slurp can also be performed in a forwards-backwards movement and is best seen side on by the audience.

On the grid, the slurp is written in the half-beat square before the actual landing on the beat. Where the word 'slurp' is written, you are just sliding across to whichever side is indicated by the arrows. The following square will be marked 'toe' in both lanes to indicate the landing on the main beat. When a forwards-backwards slurp is needed, the directional arrow will be in the lane of the raised foot and 'slurp' written in lane of the dragging foot (*Fig 69*).

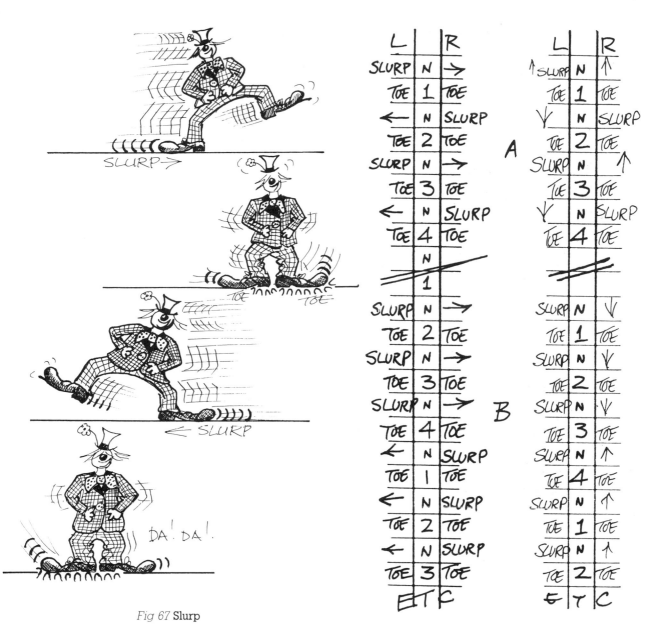

Fig 67 **Slurp**

Fig 68 (left) **Slurp,** side to side (A); and three to the right, three to the left (B)

Fig 69 (right) **Slurp,** backwards and forwards (A); and three backwards, three forwards (B)

Jump-o-foot

Jump-o-foot, preparation (toe)

Halfway through jump (jut)

Landing (toe)

As the title suggests, this is a jumping-over-your-foot step. As the R foot is brought in front of the L foot, the L foot jumps over it and lands in front. The R foot remains suspended and as still as possible. It is not quite as easy as it seems and needs careful practice in easy stages before you attempt it properly.

The first attempt should be to place the side of the toe of one foot on the floor just in front of and slightly across the other. As the back foot is lifted to come forwards over the front foot, the front foot can take a lot of the weight. This just gives you the feel of the step. The idea is to be able to perfect this jump whilst keeping the front foot off the ground. The back foot hops over it. It is also possible to hop back over it again, thereby keeping the one foot still, in suspension, whilst hopping over it forwards and backwards as many times as you wish.

You will not be able to perform this step easily to begin with but, like all the other more difficult steps, it will become easier and easier until you will think nothing of it.

The jump-o-foot can also be a very athletic step if the front leg is swung up in front and the back leg has to leap over it. Only try this when you are very confident of the less energetic version.

The grid name for the jump-o-foot is 'jut'. When written in the R lane, it means the R foot is doing the jump over and vice versa for the L foot. The take-off and landing will both be 'toe' with the 'jut' in-between: Toe-jut-toe(R) toe-jut-toe(L). (*Fig 71.*)

81

Fig 70 **Jump-o-foot**

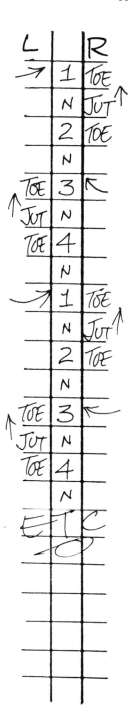

Fig 71 **Jump-o-foot**

Dig-toe-ca-toe

A hip-swivelling step with arms held up in flamenco style, the dig-toe-ca-toe stays in one spot. This time, it is all right to look down at your feet, but do it with style. Don't just slump forward as if you have a broken neck – turn your head to the side and look down past your shoulder. The breakdown of the step goes like this:

1 Dig with the R heel in front of the L foot, the R foot facing over to 11 o'clock.
2 L foot 'toe' down without moving position.
3 Ca with the R foot pulling it back in line with the L foot.
4 R foot 'toe' down beside L foot.
5 Dig with the L heel in front of the R foot, the L foot facing over to 1 o'clock.
6 R foot 'toe' down without moving position.
7 Ca with the L foot pulling it back in line with the R foot.
8 L foot 'toe' down beside R foot.

This movement can be repeated as often as you like. (*For grid, see Fig 72.*) When moving from left to right and back, the head can follow the foot that performs the dig, eg: R foot dig towards 11 o'clock, head turned to left looking down front of left shoulder; L foot dig towards 1 o'clock, head follows round and looks down front of right shoulder. Arms remain above head as if at gun point!

This movement can also be adapted to the 'tapioca' step. Instead of making it a straight-forward dig-ca-toe-he(R) towards 1 o'clock, start the 'dig' towards 11 o'clock, then during the ca-toe-he bring it back into line next to the L foot. Likewise, start the L dig off towards 1 o'clock and bring it back.

Each time the dig moves across in front, the corresponding hip should swivel around towards the front. This can be a very effective step once you get the correct feel and style.

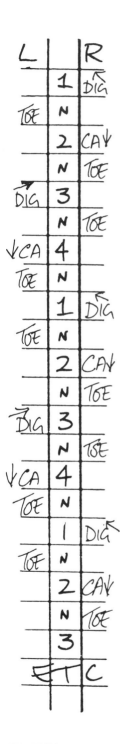

Fig 72 **Dig-toe-ca-toe**

Cutaway

This step is fairly involved but very showy. Each stage must be prepared slowly in the mind and then transmitted to the feet. Once you are sure of what you are supposed to do, it is much easier to progress with your practice. Arms are also important to give this step style (*see Fig 73*).

First, the feet. It is possible to start with either foot.

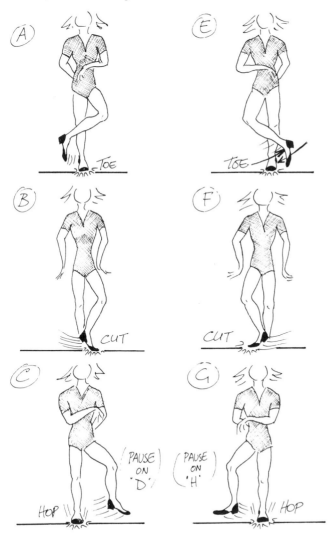

Fig 73 **Cutaway**

We will start with a 'left' cutaway:

A Hop on R foot. At same time, lift L foot up in front, toe pointing downwards. L foot remains suspended and prepares to swing left.

B L foot swings to left, across front of R foot, tip of toe catching floor as it passes through.

C L foot continues to move out sideways as far as is comfortable. (If you are *very* loose, not *too* far.) At the same time, the R foot hops again.

D This is a 'pause'. (No beat.) Whilst the L foot seems to be still, it must prepare to swing back behind the R foot.

E Reverse the procedure. L foot lands behind R foot as R foot is picked up in front, toe facing downwards, prepares to swing to right.

F R foot swings to right, across front of L foot, catching toe on floor and continues to swing right.

G Hop on L foot as R foot continues to swing out (not *too* far).

H Wait for a beat to go by whilst preparing R foot for swing back behind L foot. Continue from A. (*For the grid see Fig 74.*)

The arms are important to this step and I suggest two alternatives:

1 As at letter B, L foot is performing the cutaway, left arm swings backwards and right arm swings loosely in front of the chest. As the cutaway is transferred to the R foot (letter F) the right arm swings behind and the left arm swings up loosely in front of the chest. This is not a rigid arm movement, but neither is it sloppy. The happy-go-lucky feel between the two is good. Don't look down at your feet.

2 The other way is to hold your arms up above your head and watch your feet! As the cutaway moves from side to side, follow it with your head. Don't slouch forward or the step will lose dignity and vitality. Keep your back straight and look down at your cutaways with style and admiration.

You may discover other arm positions which look good; this is one of the thrilling bonuses. To invent your own moves and steps is extremely rewarding and opens up the ever-present possibility of developing a new style of dance which could be advantageous to everyone.

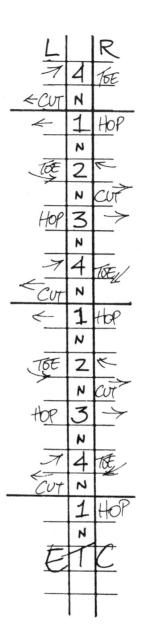

Fig 74 **Cutaway**

Cutaway (R). Hop on L foot, swing R foot across and in front of L foot

R foot swings back and is put down behind L foot which swings up in front of dropped R foot

Cut(R)

Cut(L)

Hop(L) as R foot swings outwards

Hop(R) as L foot swings outwards

Cutaway-ca

The ca can be an interesting addition to the cutaway. It is not necessary to use it every time, but included on certain occasions, it is very effective. As the suspended foot is pulled back behind as in letter E of the cutaway (page 83), try a ca before it is dropped behind.

The first two cutaways should be ordinary ones (without the ca), then the next two can include the ca: ie cutaway(L), cutaway(R), cutaway-ca(L), cutaway-ca(R) and so on.

A good way to wrap up the cutaway sequence is to perform the cutaway step without observing the pause as the cutaway foot is suspended at the side (letter D). Bring the foot back down behind on the very next beat after the hop. The timing is quite intricate as it seems to cut across the beat but if you stick with it, everything works out well with the pu'toe-da-da at the end. *For the grid, see Fig 75.*

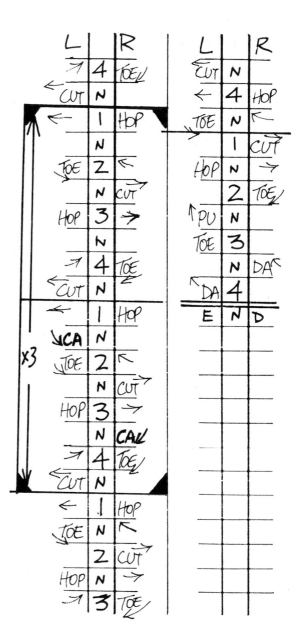

Fig 75 **Cutaway-ca**

Double-ca

This is a double jump backwards, collecting a catchback with each toe. The ca can be both feet in unison or one foot slightly after the other (staggered). In the first case, two beats are effected; in the second, four beats.

There are a few ways of launching the double-ca. The first is simply to raise the toes slightly and jump backwards, collecting the two cas on the way (*Fig 76*). Another process is to jump forwards on to the heels, then do the double-ca, unison or staggered (unison – three beats, staggered – six). Finally, jump forwards on to flat feet, unison or staggered, then the double-ca.

There are also many permutations of these steps. A unison jump forwards (da, L and R together) followed by a staggered double-ca (DA-tiddley-pom!) (*Fig 78, A*), or a staggered dig(R) dig(L) followed by a unison double-ca (–, a one, –, a two) (*Fig 78, B*). Mix them as you wish.

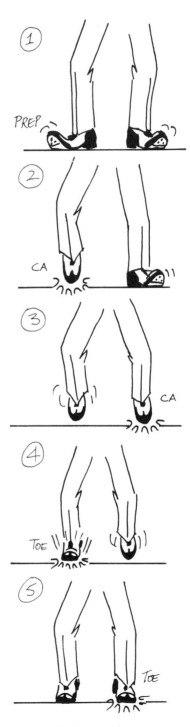

Fig 76 **Double-ca**

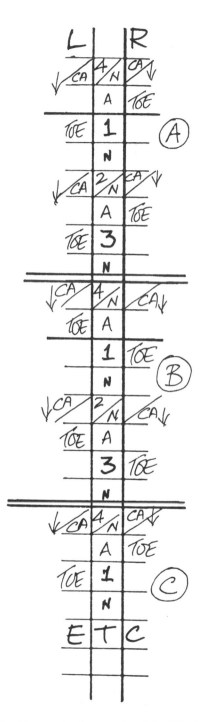

Fig 77 Double-ca, starting on the right (A), the left (B) and the right (C)

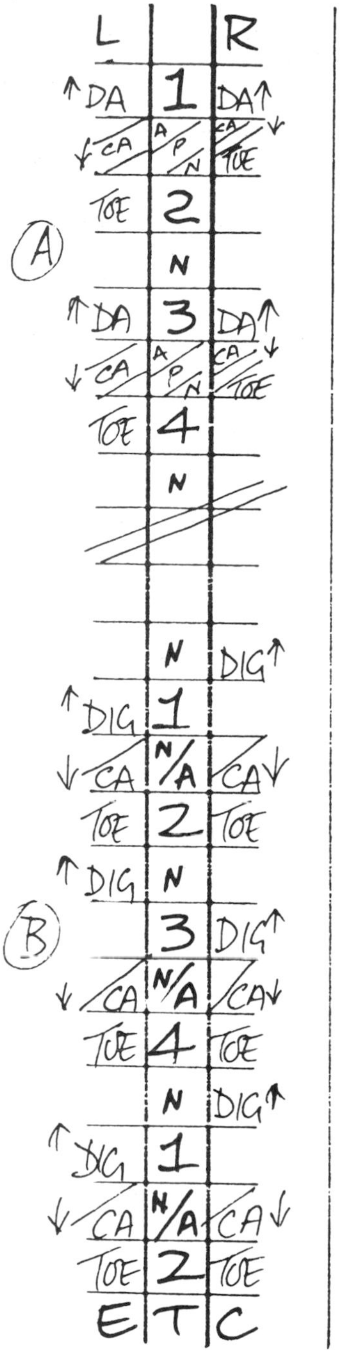

Fig 78 Double-ca variations

Extra Heel

We are now adding little subtleties here and there: for instance, the flat foot (da) can be made into a toe-heel. There are also occasions when the 'toe' can accommodate an added heel.

One step that benefits from the extra heel is da-pu'pl-ca (page 38). The da is changed into a toe-he. The beats now become so fast that it is almost impossible to chart them on the grid. A possible way is *Fig 79*. Rather cramped, but by this time you should be able to cope with it. This step was used to create the world record for the fastest tap dancing, twenty-four beats per second, on the BBC television programme, *Record Breakers*, on 14 January 1973.

Another step to benefit from the extra heel is the 'wing'. As the airborne part of the wing is completed and the toe lands, it is quite possible to then drop the heel. Again, this is very quick and rather involved on the grid, but, when performed with the pendulum wing, it is a valuable addition to the repertoire. (*see Fig 80.*)

Many opportunities arise where the toe can accommodate an extra heel and it's up to you to use it when it is going to be beneficial. Do not feel that you must cram the extra heel in at every conceivable opportunity. Often it will just clutter up the routine and lose its effect. Better to wait until you have had a fairly quiet sequence, then a little flurry helps to give your performance light and shade. At all times be aware of the rhythm of the steps as well as the appearance. You are a moving drummer and, as in good drumming, it is often what you leave out that can be extremely effective. A pause can sometimes be more dramatic than a long burst of continuous 'rat-tat-tat'. A good mixture makes a routine more enjoyable for yourself, and your audience.

Fig 79 Da-pupple-ca plus heel

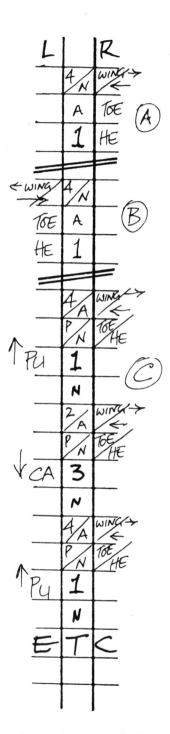

Fig 80 Wing plus heel on the right (A), on the left (B) and pendulum wing plus heel (C)

Hand-claps

The hands can be used to good effect as rhythm instruments as well as enhancing the appearance of your dancing. The opportunities are endless and I predict the hand-clap will be used more and more in really intricate rhythmic patterns.

One use of the hands to drive you nuts is first to step out with the R foot (pu-toe), then slap your thigh (right) and thigh (left). Four beats, two with the foot and two with the hands. Follow straight on with the L foot. This time, after the pu-toe(L), slap your left thigh first, then your right. You will have trouble with this until your brain has sorted it out, then it will gradually become easier and easier. It is a most delightful movement once you can perform it without a grim, determined look on your face. The beats should all be equal in length so that pu'toe-slap-slap, pu'toe-slap-slap, should sound 'n, 1, n, 2, n, 3, n, 4'. Use this first of all as an

exercise, then put it into a routine.

Another famous use of the hand-clap leaves out the feet altogether. Imagine you are standing in a square box, and on every 'off' beat in the rhythm clap first to the top-right corner, then top-left, then bottom-right, and bottom-left. It doesn't matter which side you start, or whether you start top or bottom, but if you are dancing with a partner or group, it's a good idea to all go the same way! (Unless, of course, you find this disadvantageous to your particular visual effect.) The movement looks best when the hand-claps are performed at full stretch.

An invented step of mine has quite good picture value as well as being good rhythmically. Try it.

Start facing 9 o'clock (left).
1 Pu-he(R). Foot remains suspended.
2 He(L). R foot remains suspended up front.
3 Two hand-claps, the first one under the suspended knee, and the second one above it. The hands continue in an upwards movement as:

Hand claps (my step), under . . .

. . . then above suspended knee

4 R foot comes down a pace forwards (still facing 9 o'clock). Hands fully extended.
5 Pu-he(L). Foot remains suspended.
6 He(R).
7 Di'toe(L). (Note: Di' is abbreviation for dig).
8 He(R), he(L), move to face front.
9 Da(R), move to face 3 o'clock (right). Bring hands down ready for next move.

The step is then repeated using the opposite feet. The step can be performed from side to side as often as you like. One of the main parts from a picture point of view is the hand movement following the second hand-clap. After the clap, they must travel up in front of the face together, then part company as in the brush step but once they have reached full height, they stay there until the final da. The back is bent for the two hand-claps but must straighten as the hands reach up. You can see it on the grid in *Fig 81*.

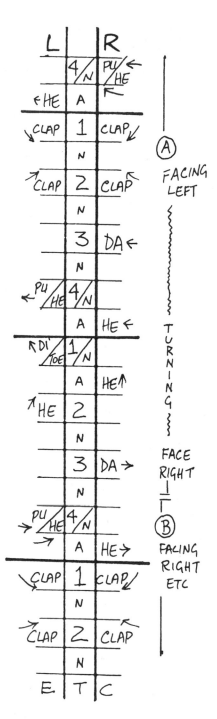

Hands continue upwards until fully extended, foot comes down a pace forward

Fig 81 **Hand-claps facing left (9 o'clock) (A) and facing right (3 o'clock) (B)**

Walking Steps

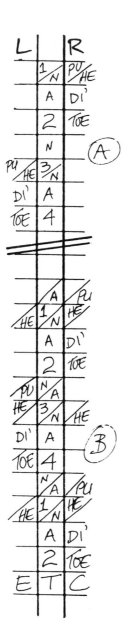

Fig 82 **Walking steps, four beats (A) and five beats (B)**

Casual in appearance, the walking steps can baffle your audience. The taps appear to be coming from nowhere. The basic step gives you four beats with each pace forwards. It can be fast or slow. You can perform it in grand style or throw it away with a shrug of the shoulders.

First of all, walk forwards as you would naturally; then, as you put your foot down, make the 'heel' and 'toe' two very separate beats. The 'heel' becomes 'dig' followed by 'toe' – 'dig-toe' (fast version, di-toe). The other two beats are performed before putting the heel down, a pu-he, followed by the dig-toe. The whole step for one pace forward is pu'he-dig-toe (fast version, pu'he-di'toe). Four equal beats sounding like tiddley-POM, the fourth beat landing on the main beat, tiddley-ONE tiddley-TWO, or pu'he-di'TOE(R) pu'he-di'TOE(L) etc. The photograph shows the actual movement with the help of a fast-blinking strobe light. First the toe catches, then follows through whilst the heel catches and continues forwards and is put down, taking the weight. The toe is put down as the other foot is raised, ready to start the step on the other side. This movement should be practised until you just appear to be walking normally. Try to avoid looking down. Look your audience straight in the face as if to say, 'What about *this*!' Then you hit them with the *five*-beat walk.

The extra beat is inserted in the middle of the four-beat walk. After you have done the pu-he with one foot and it is travelling forwards, you snatch a quick 'heel' on the grounded foot. Pu-he(R) he(L) di-toe(R). The rhythm is moved forwards slightly and sounds like 'a-tiddley-ONE, a-tiddley-TWO' etc. The main emphasis is still on the last (now fifth) beat.

Once these two walking steps are in your grasp and looking good, we can attempt the *eight*-beat walk! When perfected, this step is really fast and is the main step I used to squeeze the million taps into twenty-four hours, averaging eleven beats per second.

First three beats are pu'he-pl(R). Notice the pl, meaning the step doesn't move forwards at this point. Next we add the he(L). This is the only beat out of the eight that is performed on the other foot. The right foot then continues forwards with the ordinary four-beat walking step. As the eighth

beat is struck, the other foot should be prepared to continue with no break in the even rhythm. The eight beats should all be exactly the same time duration as each other. 'One-a-penny-two-a-penny' takes you one pace forwards and would take up 1-a-p-n-2-a-p-n, on the grid.

The arms for the basic four-beat walk are as in normal walking style, opposite arm to leg. You can, of course, invent your own arm movements, hands in pockets, arms folded, clasped behind your back, anything that feels and looks good.

The five-beat walk looks fine in the normal walking style, but is open to invention, as is the eight beat. A suggestion for the eight is the gliding position.

Arms in gliding position

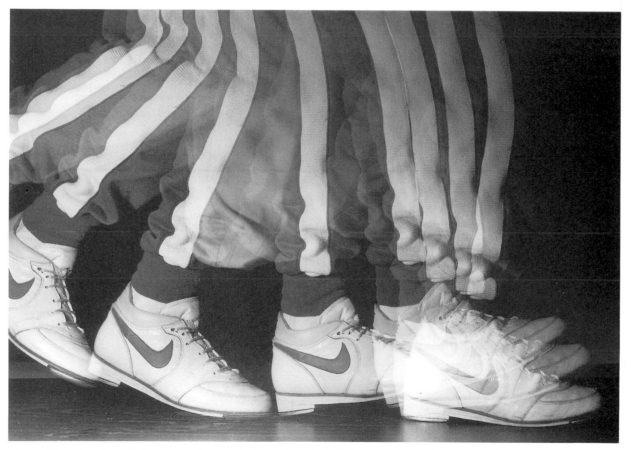

The walking step (from left): toe catches and follows through (pu); heel catches and moves on (heel); heel is put down (dig); toe is put down (toe)

Four-side

Energy time! Have a towel handy for this one. First we will perform the basic movement which is in itself a most attractive step, then we will add some extra taps to it. First, the basic movement:

1 Hop(L). R foot swings behind with bent knee. This should now form the figure '4' to your audience.

2 Hop(L). This second hop should take the L foot slightly sideways to the left whilst the R foot kicks out to the right side.

3 Toe(R). R foot swings down front centre as L foot swings behind to mirror the figure '4' as in step 1.

4 Hop(R). Hop takes R foot slightly sideways to the right whilst the L foot kicks out to the left side. L foot is then swung back to repeat the movement in step 1.

The body faces front throughout the whole of this step. The arm movement is again energetic, but essential to the style and vitality of the step. As the leg kicks outwards, the arms are swung outwards; as the legs form the figure '4', the straight arms swing and cross in front of the body. The movement should close up for the '4' then open up for the 'side'. This step is given its full visual appeal when you remember to make that second hop move slightly sideways as the other foot kicks out. Both feet moving outwards then inwards together with the corresponding arm movements is the selling feature (*Fig 83a A*).

We can now add some taps to the 4-side step:

1 Da(L). The hop is changed to a flat foot da, toe facing 10 o'clock. R foot prepares to pu'pl towards 3 o'clock.

2 Pu'pl(R) towards 3 o'clock.

3 Toe(R). R toe down in front of L as L foot is pulled behind R foot.

4 Toe(L). L toe is dropped behind R (*Fig 83a B*). The movement is then reversed and repeated as often as you wish. Remember to face forwards throughout. Arms are the same as the basic step. Now we get to a fairly difficult addition. In step 2/3, pu'pl-toe(R), as the R foot is moving towards centre after the pu'pl and is still airborne the L

foot performs a hotch (ca) and is also airborne. The R foot then finishes the original step with toe down, front centre; then the L foot finishes *its* original move of toe down, back centre. Legs crossed as before. In short, as the L foot moves from the da back to centre, it snatches a ca on the way. The timing of this ca is between the pu'pl and the toe of the R foot. This is quite an involved piece of explanation, so read it carefully until it is fully understood, then give it a whirl. The rhythm of this move is 'a, 1, n, a, 2, –, a, 3, n, a, 4-'. The 'a' between 'n' and two, and 'n' and four, is the double beat of the newly acquired ca(L) and the toe(R) – 'a, 1, n, A, 2, –, a, 3, n, A, 4' (*Fig 83a C*). This may take time to master so don't expect results straightaway. You may discover different arm movements for this final step. Opposite arms to legs is also possible.

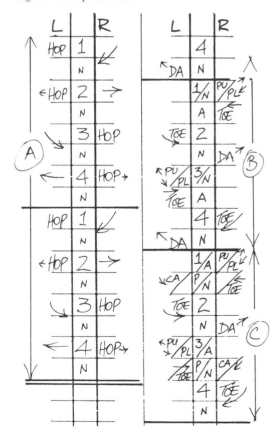

Fig 83a Four-side (A), four-side with pu'pl (B) and four-side with pu'pl ca (C)

Fig 83b **Four-side (left column) and four-side with taps (right column)**

Hupple

Occasionally, it is necessary to hop on to one foot whilst starting the pu'pl with the other. The hop(R) and pu(L) happen at exactly the same moment, then the L foot continues with the pl. First of all, try an ordinary hop(R) pu'pl-toe(L), each step separately (four beats), then try it with the hop(R) and the pu(L) together (three beats). To make this a more satisfying step, add a final toe(R), the whole move now having four beats.

This step can be repeated quite a few times by changing feet alternately. The emphasis can be either on the first beat (hop-pu) or the last beat (toe). 'Hop-pu' is two syllables and, as the two steps are danced simultaneously, we need a one syllable word to fit in with the rhythm of the step. If we merge the two words, we get 'hup', one syllable meaning both steps together. On the grid (*Fig 84*), it is possible to write the hop in one lane and the pu in the corresponding square in the other lane. Hup is used when 'talking' the routine, 'hup-pl' incorporates the three moves in two syllables.

In the possible but unlikely event of having to hop and ca at the same time, we will name it 'HA'. (grid: hop, R lane; ca, L lane.)

L		R
↑PU	1	HOP
↓PL	N	
TOE	A	
	2	TOE
	N	
	A	
HOP	3	PU↗
	N	PL↘
	A	TOE
TOE	4	
	N	
	A	
↑PU	1	HOP
↓PL	N	
TOE	A	
	2	TOE
	N	
	A	
HOP	3	PU↗
	N	PL↘
	A	TOE
TOE	4	

Fig 84 **Hupple**

Shuffle-off-to-Buffalo

One of the most famous comedy exit steps in the world of dance, 'shuffle-off' is the step, when mentioned, that brings a smile to the face of the professional tappers and, when performed, a smile to the face of your audience. It has a cheeky style, steeped in tradition and nostalgia and guarantees applause when performed well.

When you are going to exit right, the R foot starts the proceedings:

1 Toe(R).
2 Pu'pl-toe(L), towards 10 o'clock.
3 Left toe drops down behind the R foot which is lifted up across and in front of L foot to around knee height. These two moves happen simultaneously.
4 Toe(R). R foot drops to floor and takes full weight as L foot kicks out sideways towards 9 o'clock. Body faces front throughout. These last two moves are repeated until you have exited stage right.

The arm movement is also very light-hearted and accepted as an integral part of the traditional step. As the right leg is raised in front of the L foot drop (step 3), the bent right arm swings up in front of the right shoulder, fist clenched and thumb fully extended, pointing to the right. As the right leg drops, the right arm drops; as the right leg is raised, the right arm is raised. They work together throughout. The left arm remains fairly rigid down the left side of the body. This step will confuse you a little until you get the hang of it, then you will begin to enjoy it. You should appear to be almost toppling over in whichever direction you are travelling.

The step is reversed when you need to exit Left. The golden rule is to remember 'exit right, step off on right foot' and vice versa.

The timing of the step starts on beat four with the toe, followed very quickly by the pu'pl-toe of the other foot. The toe lands on the first beat of the next bar, so toe(R) pu'pl-TOE(L) equals '4, n, a, ONE'! From here on, alternate feet land on each full beat of the bar until you have exited. Check it on the grid (*Fig 86*).

Fig 85 **Shuffle-off-to-Buffalo**

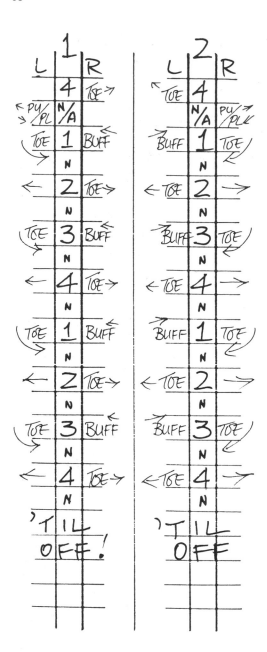

Fig 86 **Shuffle-off-to-Buffalo going right (grid 1) and going left (grid 2)**

Shuffle-off-to-Buffalo, exiting stage right. Left toe drops down behind R foot which is lifted up across and in front of L foot around knee height. (*opposite*) Toe(R). R foot drops to floor and takes full weight as L foot kicks out sideways. These two moves are continued until you have exited stage right

Dig-drag

Used frequently in eccentric routines, the dig-drag is a very light-hearted, comic step. It is a lateral movement from side to side.

1 The preparation is a double-footed jump, the legs assuming the frog position. Shoulders hunched and arms straight down by sides where they remain.

2 The L foot drops and takes the weight: the R foot remains suspended and prepares to straighten sideways.

3 R foot reaches out towards 3 o'clock and 'digs' at full stretch. Shoulders drop.

4 As the R foot digs, the weight is transferred to the right side and the L foot drags along the floor and is then placed behind the R foot. As the weight moves over to the R foot, the dig levels into a flat foot and the heel is raised by the time the L foot is put down behind. At this point the legs are crossed, R foot in front, both heels raised.

5 The step is now reversed starting with the jump up (frog), shoulders hunched. R foot is dropped and L foot prepares to reach out etc.

The dig-drag can be repeated as often as you wish and looks funny when performed well. The legs are the most animated part of the step. The hunched shoulders for the frog followed by the dropped shoulders as you dig add greatly to the overall effect. High knees for the frog, and a good drag across are points to work on. The arms must remain rigidly at your side to give the legs and shoulders the star part.

Dig-drag, stage 2, R foot preparing to straighten sideways

Dig at full stretch, showing dropped shoulders (stage 3)

After the drag (stage 4), legs crossed, both heels raised

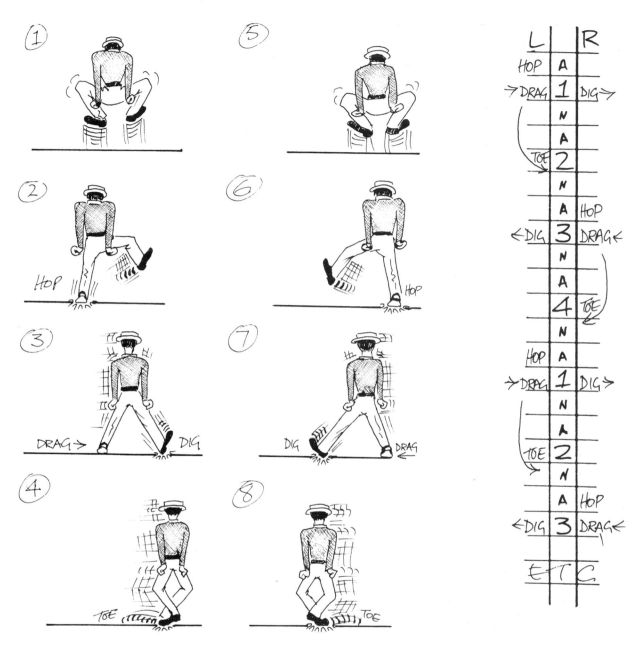

Fig 87 **Dig-drag**

Fig 88 **Dig-drag**

Gallop

A sideways movement, the gallop is a means of getting a heel klik as weight is transferred from one foot to the other. When the step is moving left towards 9 o'clock (the body is facing forwards), the L foot reaches out and 'toe' is put down a pace to the side. The weight is then transferred to the L foot as the R foot is picked up and is brought towards the stationary L foot. Before the R foot is put down beside the L foot, the L foot takes off again, the R foot 'kliks' heels and is put down ('toe') as the L foot moves out another pace to the side to repeat the sequence as often as the routine requires. The beats are even and are usually best in rhythms using three beats: 1, n, a, 2, n, a, or toe(L) klik toe(R), toe(L) klik toe(R). This step is used in the 'soft shoe' routine.

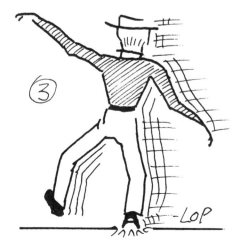

Fig 89 **Gallop**

L		R
① ←TOE	1	
②	N	GAL ←
③	A	LOP
① ←TOE	2	
②	N	GAL ←
③	A	LOP
① ←TOE	3	

Arm-clocks

In order to give a definite position for the arms, we use two imaginary clocks. The first one is the floor-clock and the second is the vertical clock.

We are already familiar with the floor-clock where directly forwards is 12 o'clock, 3 o'clock is right, 6 o'clock is directly behind and 9 o'clock is left. Once we have established the direction on the floor-clock, the vertical clock is used to confirm the height. We only need half the clock this time, so we will use 12 o'clock, directly overhead, down through 1 o'clock to 6 o'clock, straight down.

A simple example of these arm directions would be, left arm, floor-clock 9 o'clock, vertical clock 3 o'clock. Your left arm should be pointing directly left at shoulder height. Left arm, floor-clock 12, vertical clock 3 – your left arm should be pointing straight ahead at shoulder height. L arm, floor-clock 9, vertical clock 6 – your left arm should be straight down by your side. These are the simple positions, easily explained. The system can be more involved, but all movements should be 'chartable'. Here are the abbreviations:

Floor-clock	f/c
Vertical clock	v/c
12 o'clock etc	12 etc.

The abbreviated version of the right arm pointing straight upwards would be: R arm, f/c 3, v/c 12. Whichever way you are facing, on the stage, 12 o'clock (f/c) is always directly ahead of *you*. Should you wish to indicate the right arm straight out to the side, the abbreviation would be: R arm, f/c 3, v/c 3.

This is, at least, a way of suggesting the arm positions to the reader and becomes less difficult to understand with use.

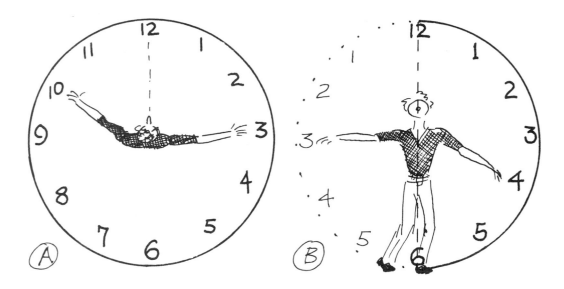

Fig 90 **Arm-clocks:** floor-clock (**A**), right arm 3 o'clock,
left arm 10 o'clock, right arm position f/c 3, v/c 3;
vertical clock (**B**), right arm 3 o'clock, left arm 4
o'clock, left arm position f/c 10, v/c 4

Arm clocks: R arm, f/c 3, v/c 4; L arm, f/c 9, v/c 1

R arm, f/c 3, v/c 3; L arm, f/c 12, v/c 3

Soft shoe

A great favourite of many, the soft shoe is nice and calm – at least it must appear that way. In truth, it is no easier than any of the other tap routines, if it is performed well.

The timing in musical terms is 12/8 which means twelve beats to the bar. These are made up of four sets of triplets: 1,n,a,2,n,a,3,n,a,4,n,a. Because of this, our grid (*Fig 91a*) is changed to accommodate the count. We now have twelve squares to the bar.

The routine starts with the whispered words, 'A one, – a two, – gi'me that old soft shoe' followed by the da(R) da(L) before the start of bar 1. This da-da is small and almost thrown away in order that the next move becomes the real start of the routine (bars are numbered and ringed for easy reference):

Col 2, bar 1, sq 1: R foot steps out to the right side.
Sq 2: L foot crosses behind and toe is put down.
Sq 2,n,a: R foot steps out (right) toe down.
Sq 3: L foot crosses in front, toe down.
Sq 4: R foot fully down. This is more of a little jump on to the flat foot.
Bar 2, sq 1: L toe crosses behind again.
Sq 1,n,a: R toe steps out again.
Sq 2: L toe crosses in front again.
Sq 3: R foot fully down again with weight travelling in the direction of two o'clock ready for:
Sq 4: shunt(R). R foot hops forwards and holds position. R arm, f/c 2, v/c 2. L arm, f/c 8, v/c 4. Left leg raised behind, under left arm.
Col 3, bar 3, sq 1: Hupple. Hop on the L foot as you start the pu'pl(R). The rest of bar 3 and 4 are self-explanatory and just need working out.
Col 4, bars 5 to 8 are the same as bars 1 to 4 on the opposite feet.
Col 6, bar 9, sq 1 (*overleaf*): this is a cheeky step and warrants a bit of salesmanship. As the double pu'pl is performed three times by the R foot, the L foot is stationary. Both arms pointing left (f/c 9, v/c 3), head watching R foot. Bar 10, sq 2,n,a: look front again for the pu-toe-toe-he-he. (Arms down by sides.)
Col 7, bars 11 and 12: same thing, other side.
Col 8, bar 13, sq 1: cahitos starting with toe(R). This step moves straight back so make full use of the visual effect of the tips crossing behind in bar 14. Repeat first part of step through bar 15, then watch out for the da-das, bar 16. (cont on page 111)

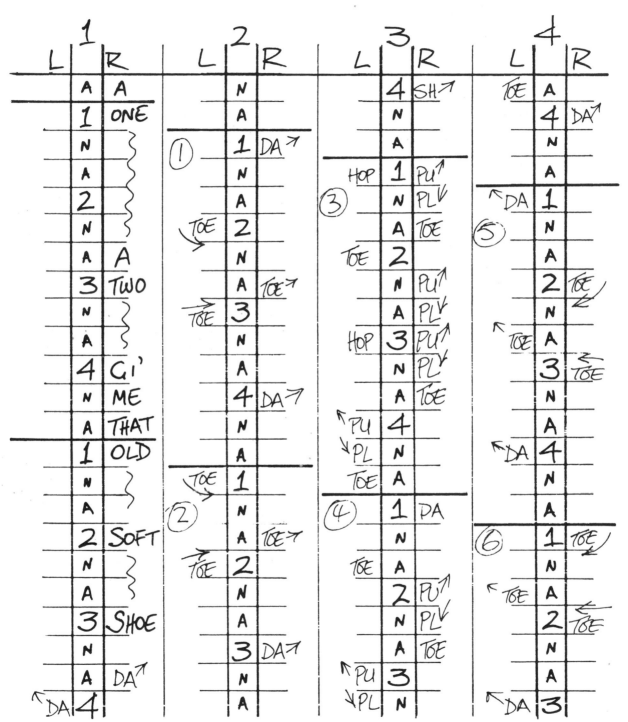

Fig 91a **Soft-shoe routine** *(beginning)*

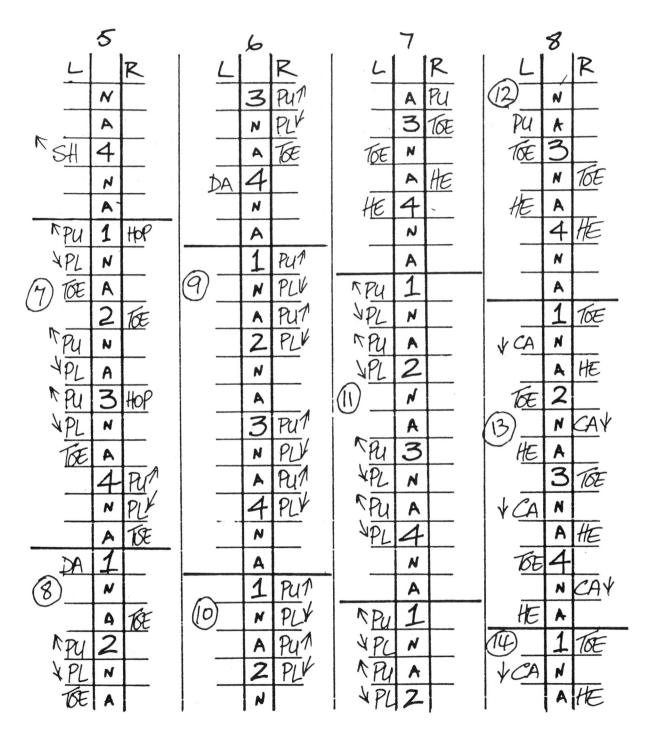

Fig 91b **Soft-shoe routine** *(cont)*

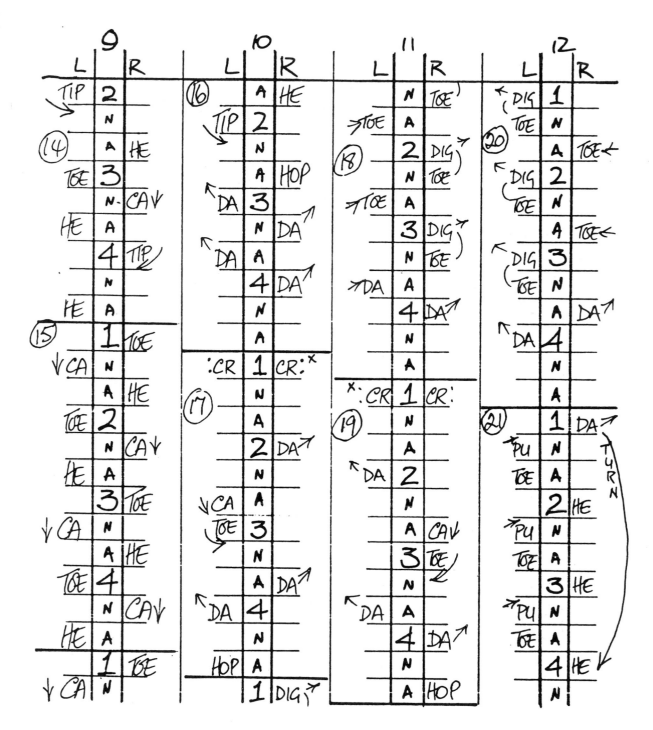

Fig 91c **Soft-shoe routine** *(cont)*

110

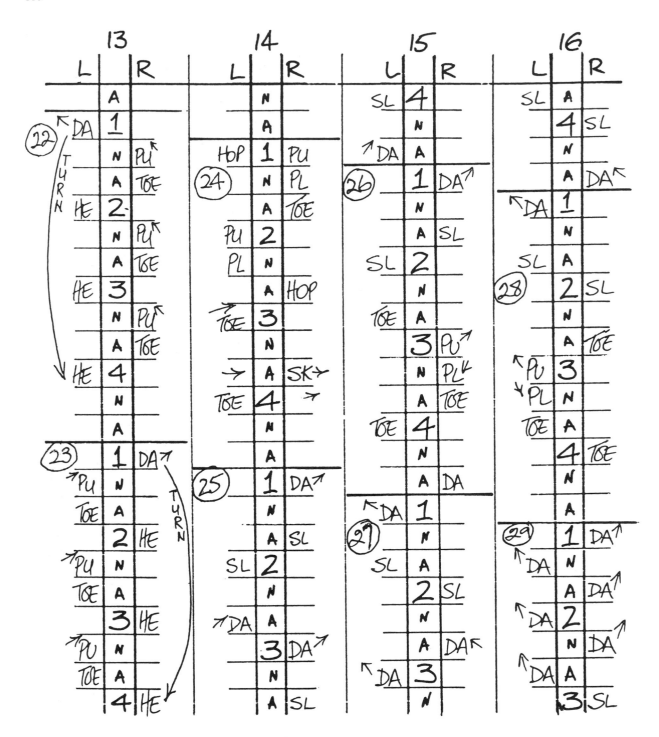

Fig 91d **Soft-shoe routine** *(cont)*

Col 10, bar 17, sq 1: cramp roll, four very quick beats, the fourth one landing *on* the beat, so this step has to be slightly anticipated. Sq 2: da(R), step out and take weight as the ca-toe(L) crosses behind. Da-da halts the movement ready for:

Col 10, bar 17, sq 4,n,a: this movement travels towards 1 o'clock and is started by the hop(L). Bar 18, sq 1: dig(R), then the right toe is dropped leaving the flat foot on the floor. Sq 1,n,a: left toe is moved towards R foot which then dig-toes towards 1 o'clock again (and again). The arms for these dig-toes are right hand around the left hip and left hand behind back. Both arms bent. Relax arm position for the da-das.

Col 11, bars 19–20: same step, other way.

Col 12, bar 21, sq 1: da(R) starts a slow turn to the right. The R foot remains grounded for the whole turn and just raises and drops heel as L foot pu-toes its way round. Each time the heel(R) is dropped, the pu-toe(L) should carry you round for a quarter turn. If the first da(R) sets off towards 3 o'clock, the following three heels(R) should bring you back to face front. Bar 22 takes you the other way and 23 takes you round to the right again.

Col 14, bar 24: starting with a hupple, the main thing to watch out for is the step across at sq 3. The L toe crosses and the R foot swings out to the right side for the side-klik (sk) sq 3,n,a. Sq 4: toe(L) drops to take weight as R foot remains suspended until:

Col 14, bar 25, sq 1: da(R) towards 2 o'clock, knees slightly bent to accommodate the thigh 'slaps' at sqs 1,n,a and 2. This is a simple slap of the thigh with the flat of the hand. The hand remains on the thigh until the next da-das. The next few bars are as they look. The final clap at sq 4 of bar 32 is the hands together in front of the face. (*cont overleaf*)

Soft shoe thigh slaps

Col 18, bar 33, sq 1: the hop(L) in the previous bar propels this dig-drag to the right, followed by the hop(R) (sq 2,n,a) which propels you back again. Once more in each direction, then steps we know well by now. This sequence is repeated starting the other way (note bar 37 is repeated).

Col 22, bar 40: the slurp is anticipated on the last beat of the previous bar so be prepared for it. The third slurp is followed by da(L) da(R) da(L) then a brush(R), sq 4. This brush is only a small one travelling towards 2 o'clock. This move to the right is continued by the hop(L), then at the start of bar 41, toe(R) steps towards 2 o'clock again as the L foot crosses behind, beginning the turn (L shoulder backwards, anticlockwise). The turn is continued by the toe(R) and toe(L) and is completed by the da(R) at sq 4. This step is repeated three times.

Col 23, bar 42: the slurp of the previous bar leads into the da(L) which in turn starts a move towards 9 o'clock. Each da steps further to the left and the ca-das(R) follow. The gallops continue in the same direction. Arms, L, f/c 9, v/c 2; R, f/c 3, v/c 4.

Col 24, bars 44–51: we now repeat the beginning of the routine (sigh of relief) and dance bars 1–8 again.

Col 28, bar 52: trenches as we are nearing the finish. First starting with the R foot forwards as the L foot slides back. Aeroplane arms for the turn in bar 53. Twice more in alternate directions, two hupple toe-toes in bar 58, then a simple finish:

Bar 59, sq 1: pu(R) is a long one out towards 2 o'clock, pl(R) is swung back across L foot and tip(R) is put down across and in front of L foot and stays there. The head is dropped on beat 4 and is not brought up until the crowd has gone wild with delight! Take your bow with dignity and feel proud of yourself. (Alternative finishing positions are shown on page 117.)

Good tunes for the soft shoe are *The Shadow of Your Smile, Tea for Two, Two Sleepy People* and *Me and My Shadow*. Many of the other four-beat tunes suggested for other routines can be used for the soft shoe if slowed down. They need the twelve-beats-to-a-bar feel.

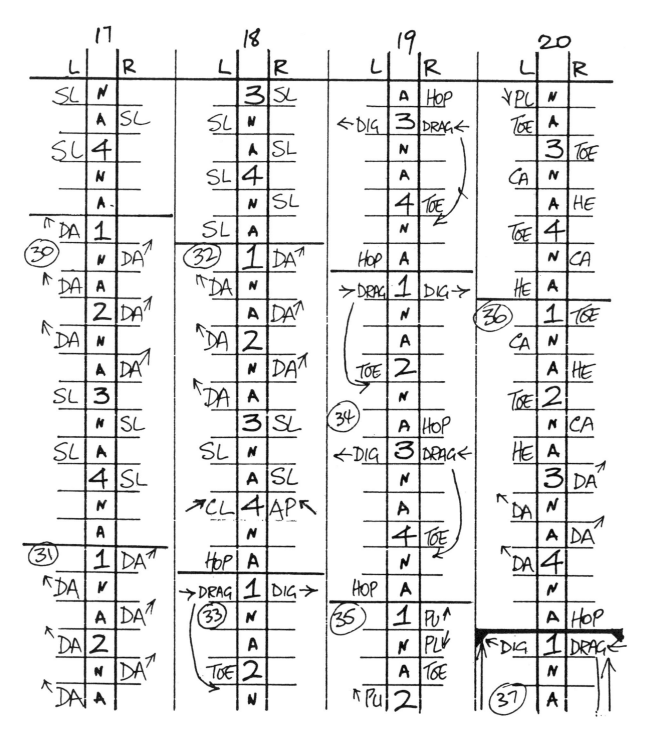

Fig 91e **Soft-shoe routine** *(cont)*

114

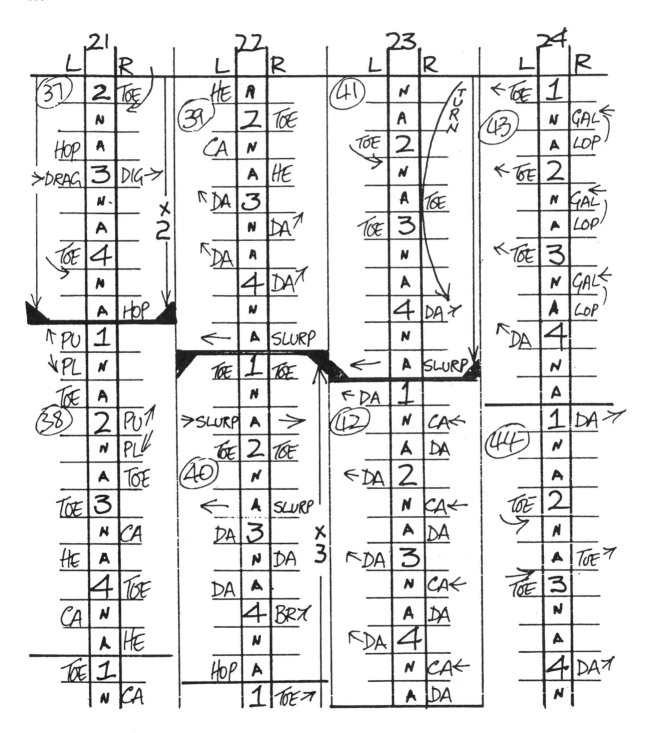

Fig 91f **Soft-shoe routine** *(cont)*

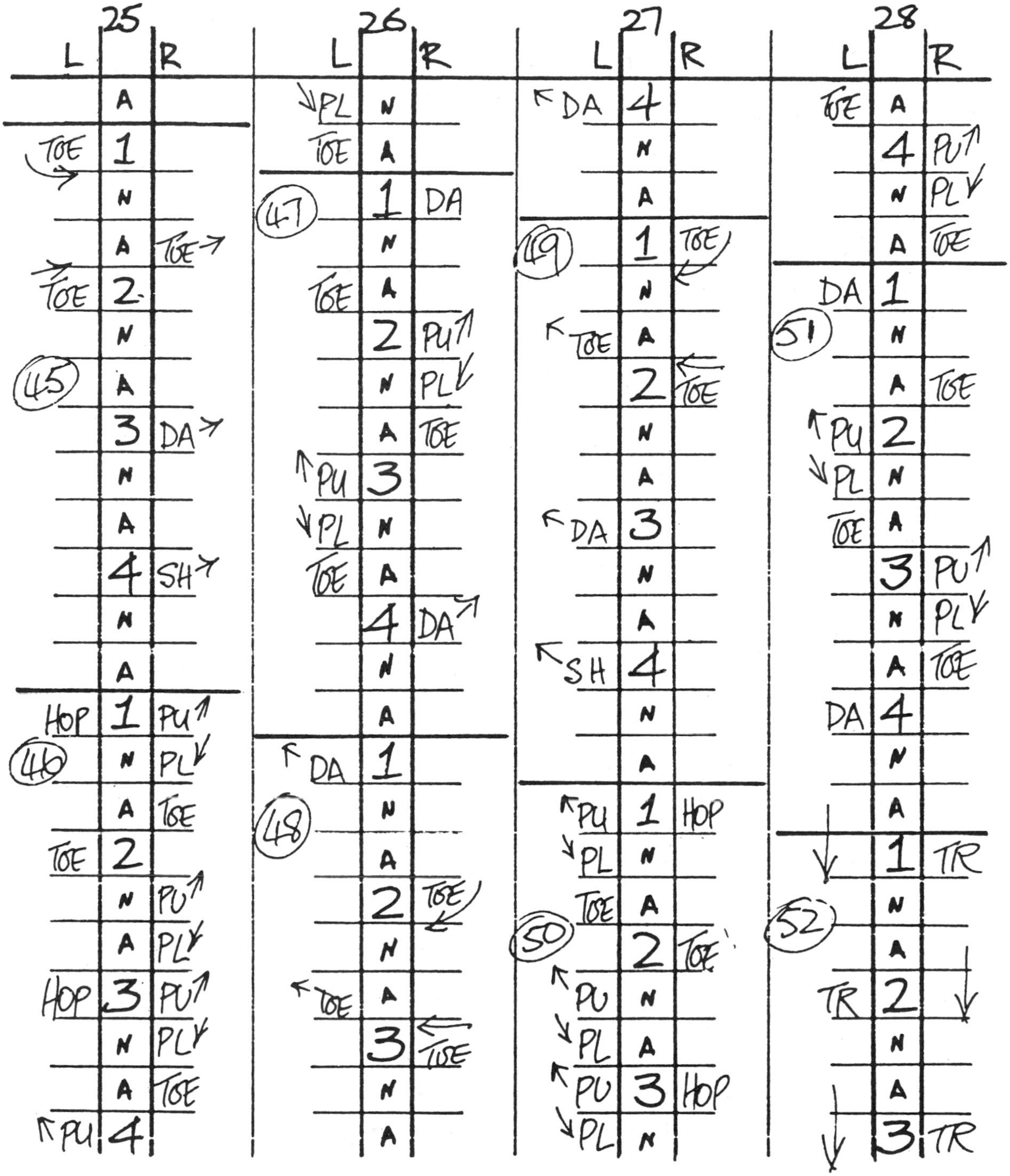

Fig 91g **Soft-shoe routine** *(cont)*

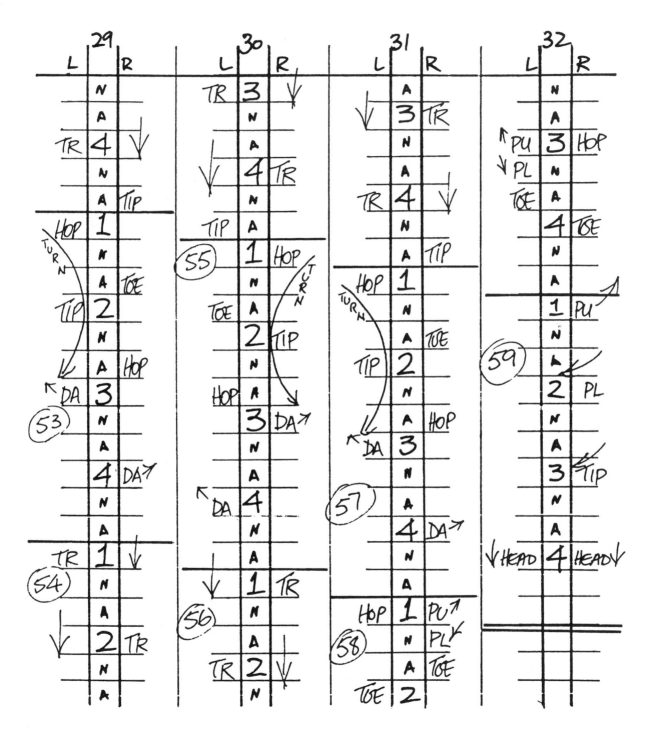

Fig 91h **Soft-shoe routine** *(end)*

Alternative finishing positions for soft shoe
routine. If you're not wearing a hat, hands
should be as in top picture

Three Beat Treat

There are many occasions when you will have to tap dance to a waltz tempo (three beats to the bar). It can be a fast waltz or a slow one, jazz or floaty-floaty. In the following routine (*Fig 92*), we can make good use of cahito and side-klik. Read it through and compare it with the grid until you fully understand the moves, then work them out slowly, gradually becoming sure of what you are doing; then you can work on your performance and style. The feel should be a happy, snappy, carefree one. Don't look down at your feet, remember your face has to dance too! The introduction music can be as long as you wish, in this case, we have allowed two bars.

Col 1, bar 1, sq 2,n: after the pu'pl(R), the R foot crosses in front and is put down (toe), then toe(L) crosses behind a little further (towards 3 o'clock). Bar two, the movement is reversed.

Col 2, bar 3: L toe steps even further across to the right as the R foot swings out to the side. This swing takes up the squares of n,2 then the side klik(R) is performed on the count of '2,n'. L foot landing immediately afterwards on the count of 3, R foot remaining suspended. This side-klik can be big or small according to your own particular athletic desires. Bar 4 is a repetition of the side-klik to the left. These first four bars are repeated three times.

Bars 5 and 6 are the same as 1 and 2.

Col 3, bar 7: toe(L) brush(R) hop(L) all facing front. Bar 8: the R foot is slammed down towards 1 o'clock and arms both forwards, palms up. Hold this position for the whole four counts, head up.

Bar 9: this is the cahito step starting on the toe. Watch the timing here. The L foot takes all the main beats (first beat of each bar), then continues to lead the da-das in bar 12. Really enjoy these da-das!

Col 4, bar 13: cahito sequence repeated with the main beats taken on the R foot. (*cont overleaf*)

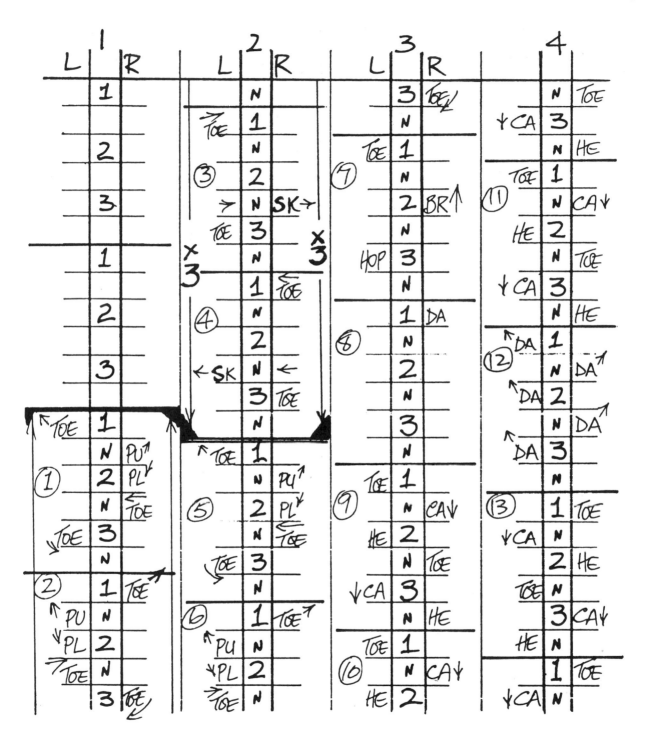

Fig 92a **Three beat treat** *(beginning)*

Col 5, bar 17: same again with emphasis back on the L foot.

Col 6, bars 21 and 22: cahito R emphasis until:

Bar 23: sequence is broken by the L foot tip behind at sq 2,n, and again at sq 2, bar 24 (R foot). This comes as a surprise at first. A few runs at it and you will enjoy the way everything finally fits. At this point, you should have completed one chorus of a thirty-two bar sequence – *I'm Forever Blowing Bubbles* for instance.

Col 7, bar 25: here we jump forward with both feet at the same time, landing on flat feet (da), then the double ca, R foot first, landing on toes (R first). This step is performed three times to the end of bar 27, then brush(L) (bar 28) is a short one towards 11 o'clock. Note the timing of this brush.

Col 8, bar 29: sequence repeated with the br (bar 32) on the R foot this time.

Col 9, bars 33–36: same again br(L).

Col 10, bars 37–40: repeat of bars 21–24.

Cols 11 and 12, bars 41–44: almost a repeat of the opening four bars except the side-klik is performed first, then the pu'pl step. The four bars are repeated three times before the final da-br-hop-DA! (bar 47). As the last da is the end, make it a good strong one. Your audience must be left in no doubt as to whether or not you have finished.

Good tunes for this one are *Edelweiss*, *Anniversary Waltz* and *Charmaine*. If you're making your own music, many four-beat tunes can be 'doctored' into a three-beat feel by an average musician.

121

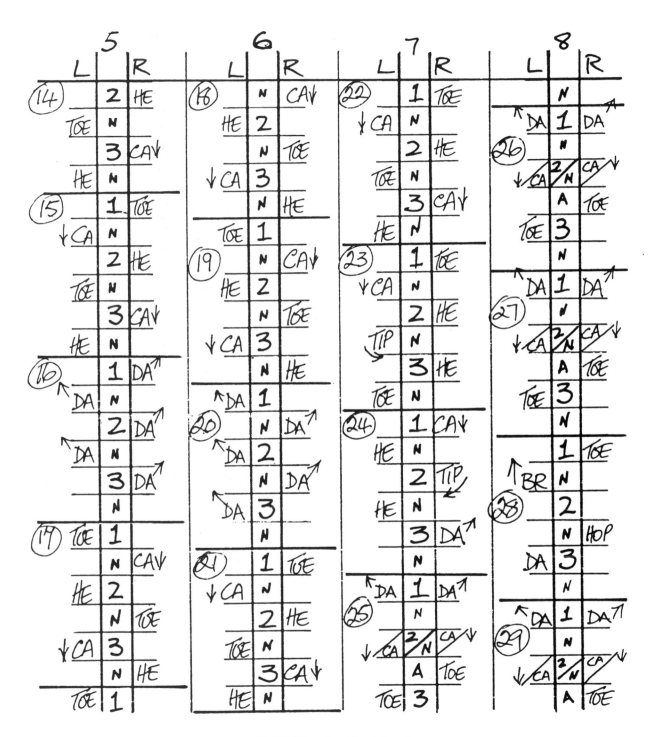

Fig 92b **Three beat treat** *(cont)*

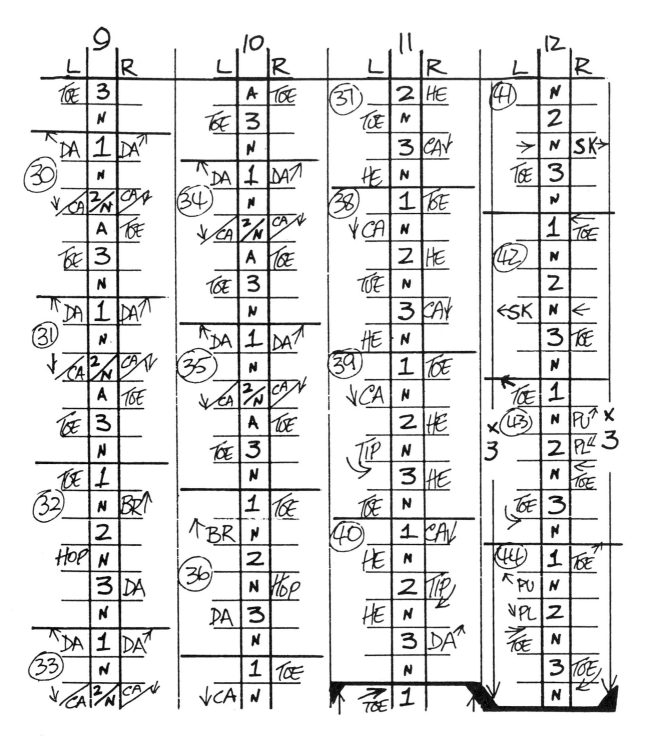

Fig 92c **Three beat treat** *(cont)*

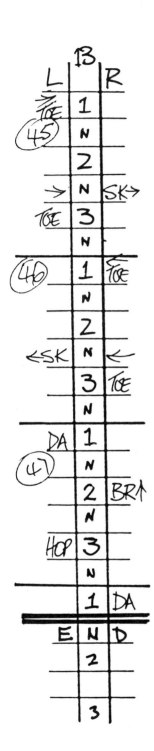

Fig 92d **Three beat treat** *(end)*

Time-step Saga

This routine is a pretty good work-out and is based on the time step. (*For grids see Fig 93.*) The introduction can be as long or short as you like, as long as you start with the pu'pl(R) in the 4 and 4-n squares before the main theme begins.

Col 1: we begin with the single time-step through bars 1 and 2, then at sq 3-n the da-das move to the left and the arms are gradually raised (both pointing left, 10 o'clock, v/c). By the time you reach bar 4 (col 3) sq 4, arms should be at full height then dropped again for the hop (bar 5). The step is now repeated in the other direction.

Col 4, bar 9: same sequence using double time-step.

Col 7, bar 17: same sequence using triple time-step.

Col 10, bar 25: weight is kept mainly on L foot and step moves a little to the right. Emphasise the flat-foot da-das. Change weight to R foot as step changes direction at bar 29 (col 11).

Col 12, bar 33: this step is stationary, weight on L foot as far as sq 2, bar 34 then R foot is dropped behind the L foot. The step is reversed at bar 35 and these four bars are repeated four times. The emphasis in this step is the da after each hop.

(*cont on page 128*)

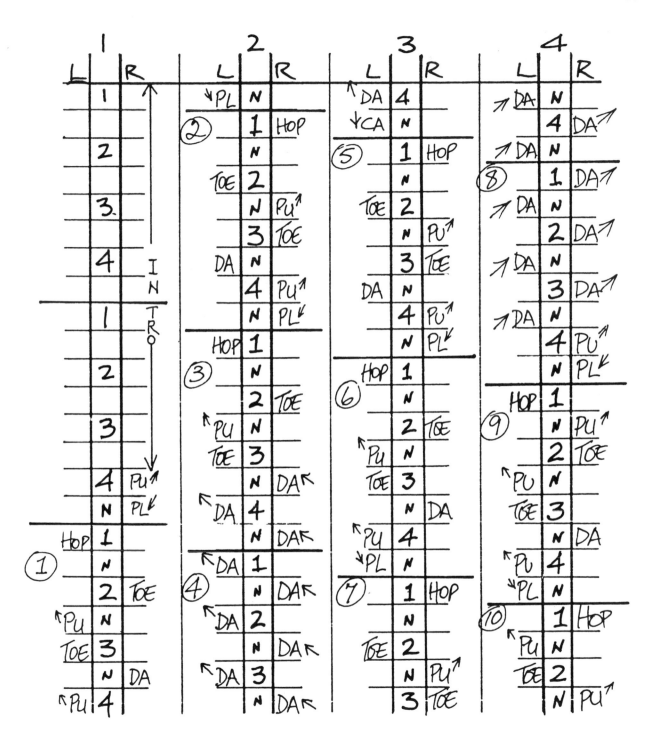

Fig 93a **Time-step saga** *(beginning)*

5

L	R	
	3	TOE
DA	N	
	4	PU↗
	N	PL↙
HOP	1	
(11)	N	PU↗
	2	TOE
↖PU	N	
TOE	3	
	N	DA↖
↖DA	4	
	N	DA↖
(12) ↖DA	1	
	N	DA↖
↖DA	2	
	N	DA↖
↖DA	3	
	N	DA↗
↗PU	4	
↘PL	N	
(13)	1	HOP
↖PU	N	
TOE	2	

6

L	R	
	N	PU↗
	3	TOE
DA	N	
	4	PU↗
	N	PL↙
HOP	1	
(14)	N	PU↗
	2	TOE
PU	N	
TOE	3	
	N	DA
PU	4	
PL	N	
(15)	1	HOP
PU	N	
TOE	2	
	N	PU
	3	TOE
↗DA	N	
	4	DA↗
↗DA	N	
	1	DA↗
↗DA	N	

7

L	R	
(16)	2	DA↗
↗DA	N	
	3	DA↗
↗DA	N	
	4	PU
	N	PL
HOP	1	
(17)	N/A	PU/PL
	2	TOE
PU	N	
TOE	3	
	N	DA
PU	4	
PL	N	
	1	HOP
PU/PL	N/A	
TOE	2	
(18)	N	PU
	3	TOE
DA	N	
	4	PU
	N	PL
HOP	1	

8

L	R	
	N/A	PU/PL
(19)	2	TOE
PU	N	
TOE	3	
	N	DA↖
↖DA	4	
	N	DA↖
↖DA	1	
(20)	N	DA↖
↖DA	2	
	N	DA↖
↖DA	3	
	N	DA↖
↖PU	4	
↘PL	N	
	1	HOP
↘PU/PL	N/A	
TOE	2	
(21)	N	PU↗
	3	TOE
DA	N	
	4	PU↗
	N	PL↙

Fig 93b **Time-step saga** *(cont)*

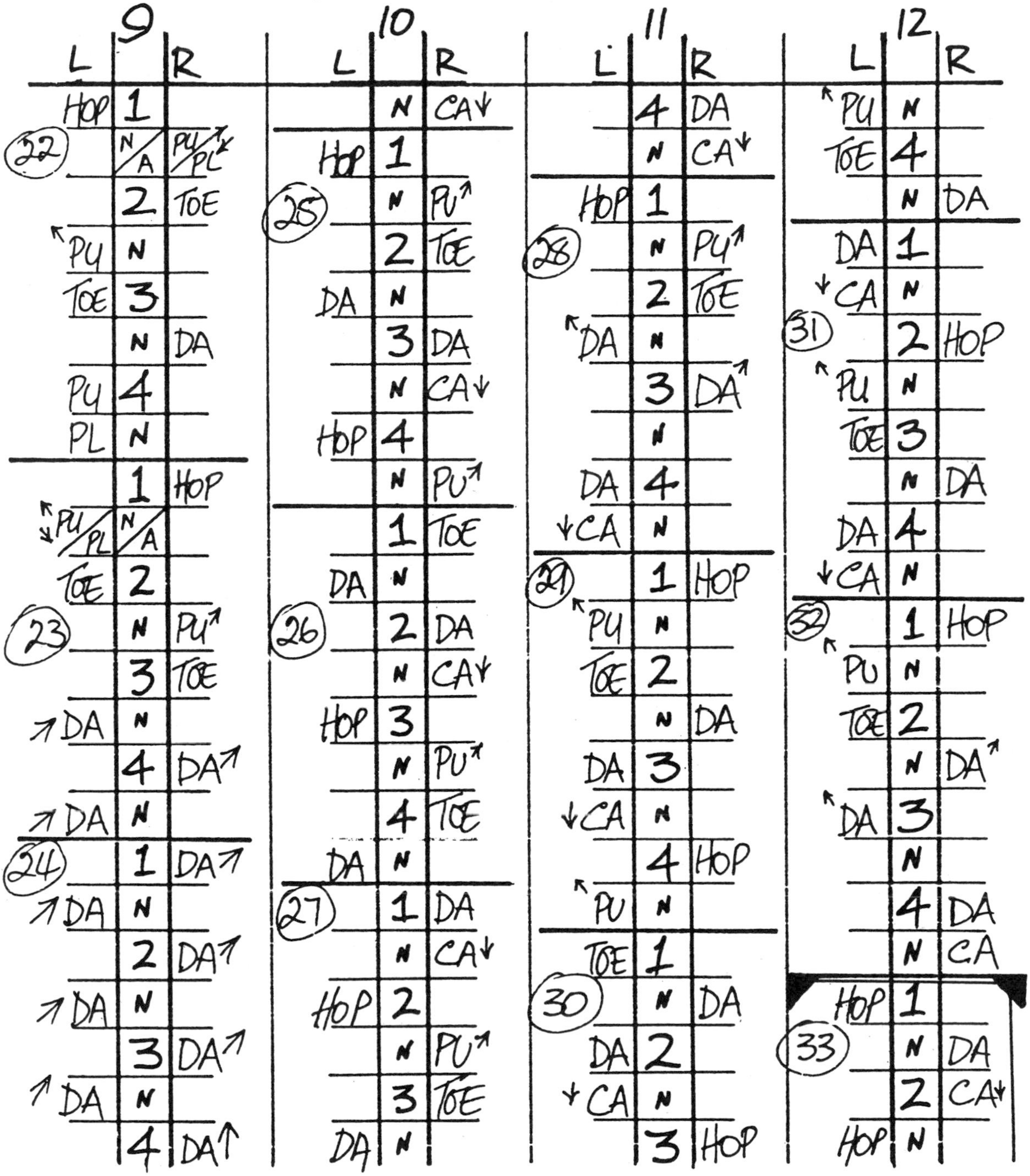

	9			10			11			12	
L		**R**	**L**		**R**	**L**		**R**	**L**		**R**
HOP	1			N	CA↓		4	DA	↖PU	N	
(22)	N/A	PU/PL↗	HOP	1			N	CA↓	TOE	4	
	2	TOE	(25)	N	PU↗	HOP	1			N	DA
↖PU	N			2	TOE	(28)	N	PU↗	DA	1	
TOE	3		DA	N			2	TOE	↓CA	N	
	N	DA		3	DA	↖DA	N		(31)	2	HOP
PU	4			N	CA↓		3	DA↗	↖PU	N	
PL	N		HOP	4			N		TOE	3	
	1	HOP		N	PU↗	DA	4			N	DA
↑↓PU/PL	N/A			1	TOE	↓CA	N		DA	4	
TOE	2		DA	N		(29)	1	HOP	↓CA	N	
(23)	N	PU↗	(26)	2	DA	↖PU	N		(32)	1	HOP
	3	TOE		N	CA↓	TOE	2		PU	N	
↗DA	N		HOP	3			N	DA	TOE	2	
	4	DA↗		N	PU↗	DA	3			N	DA↗
↗DA	N			4	TOE	↓CA	N		↖DA	3	
(24)	1	DA↗	DA	N			4	HOP		N	
↗DA	N		(27)	1	DA	↖PU	N			4	DA
	2	DA↗		N	CA↓	TOE	1			N	CA
↗DA	N		HOP	2		(30)	N	DA	HOP	1	
	3	DA↗		N	PU↗	DA	2		(33)	N	DA
↑DA	N			3	TOE	↓CA	N			2	CA↓
	4	DA↑	DA	N			3	HOP	HOP	N	

Fig 93c **Time-step saga** *(cont)*

Col 14, bar 37: this bar is repeated six times and the weight is totally on the L foot. Each hop should take you a little to the left. Stay on the spot for the triple time-step break at bars 38 and 39. Arms are as you please but I would suggest the gliding position, looking back at the pu'pling foot.

Col 15, bars 40–42: same step in other direction.

Col 16, bar 43: the quick pu'pl in squares 1-n-a and 2-n-a, are best performed behind at about 4 o'clock and each hop should take your chest a little closer to the ground. Straighten up again after the third hop in order to do the same thing when you do the three hops on the R foot at bar 45 (col 17). These four bars are repeated three times. Arms are simply dropped straight down from shoulders. Three more hops(L) at bar 47 followed by single time-step and triple break.

Col 19, bar 50, sq 4: here we repeat the single time-step as at the beginning of the routine *but*, add the ca as in time hotch step (page 37). The hotch is added to single, double and triple. Not easy!

Col 23, bar 62, sq 4: a simple clap of the hands at around shoulder height. Bar 63: hop(L) and flam(R) at the same time as in the usual flam step, repeat on other foot. Bar 65: three trenches starting with R foot forward as L foot slides back. Left arm forward with R foot etc. *Da-da* to finish and drop head on beat 4. There it is! The timing in places is quite intricate and may take a little working out but perseverance will pay handsomely.

The whole routine lasts for three choruses of a thirty-two bar melody, ie ninety-six bars in all, four beats to the bar. This is one of the work-outs that might necessitate the purchase of a towel and a change of clothes!

Good tunes would be *Putting on the Ritz, 42nd Street, Top Hat, White Tie and Tails, I've got Rhythm, Sweet Georgia Brown*, or any of the tunes listed for Alpha-beat Routine.

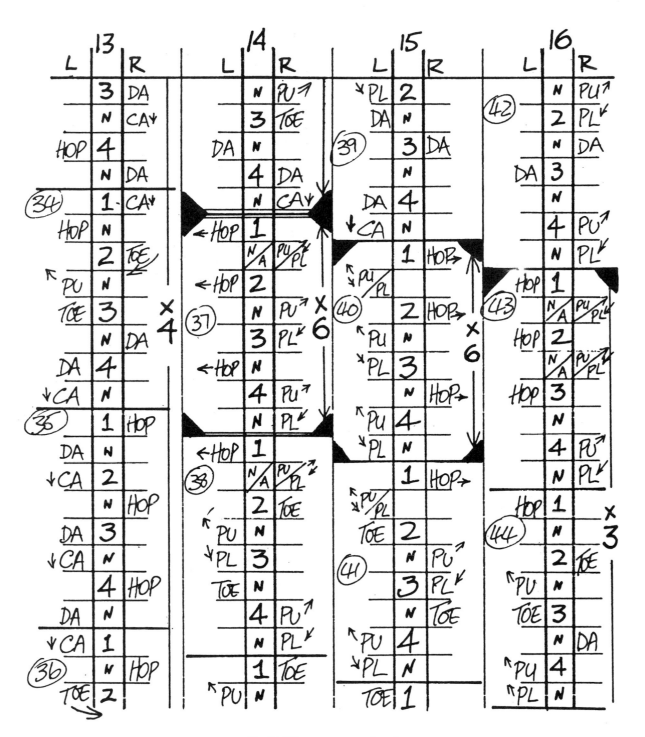

Fig 93d **Time-step saga** *(cont)*

17

L	R	
(45)	1	HOP
↗PU ↘PL / N A		
	2	HOP
↗PU ↘PL / N A		
	3	HOP
	N	
↗PU	4	
↘PL	N	
(46)	1	HOP
	N	
TOE	2	
	N	PU↗
	3	TOE
DA	N	
	4	PU↗
	N	PL↙
HOP	1	
(47) N/A	PU/PL	
HOP	2	
N/A	PU/PL	
HOP	3	
	N	
	4	PU↗

18

L	R	
	N	PL↙
HOP	1	
(48)	N	
	2	TOE
↖PU	N	
TOE	3	
	N	DA
↖PU	4	
↘PL	N	
	1	HOP
↗↘PU PL / N A		
TOE	2	
	N	PU↗
	3	PL↙
	N	TOE
↖PU	4	
↘PL	N	
TOE	1	
(50)	N	PU↗
	2	PL↙
	N	DA
DA	3	
	N	

19

L	R	
	4	PU↗
↓CA / N A / PL↙		
TOE	1	
(51)	N	
	2	TOE
↖PU	N	
TOE	3	
	N	DA
↖PU	4	
↓PL / N A / CA↓		
(52)	1	TOE
	N	
TOE	2	
	N	PU↗
	3	TOE
DA	N	
	4	PU↗
↓CA / N A / PL↙		
↓TOE	1	
(53)	N	
	2	TOE
↖PU	N	
TOE	3	

20

L	R	
	N	DA↖
↖DA	4	
	N	DA↖
↖DA	1	
(54)	N	DA↖
↙DA	2	
	N	DA↖
↖DA	3	
	N	DA↑
↖PU	4	
↙PL / N A / CA↓		
	1	TOE
↖PU	N	
TOE	2	
(55)	N	PU↗
	3	TOE
DA	N	
	4	PU↗
↓CA / N A / PL↙		
↓TOE	1	
(56)	N	PU↗
	2	TOE
↖PU	N	

Fig 93e **Time-step saga** *(cont)*

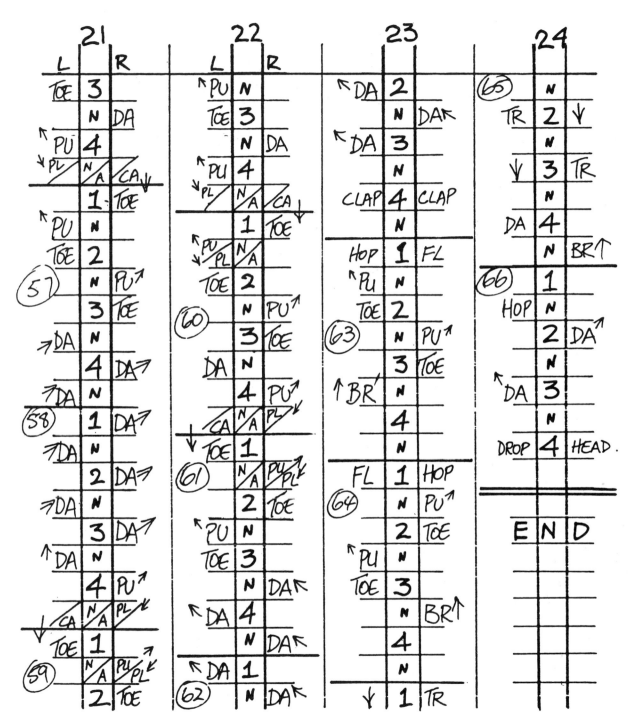

Fig 93f **Time-step saga** *(end)*

Close Beat Feat

Col 1: musical introduction – in this case, one bar and three beats. Bar 1, sq 1-n: R toe crosses in front of L foot ready for L toe to hick R heel.

Col 2, bar 4: four hops(R), arms raised about shoulder height. Right arm pointing in direction of movement, left arm opposite direction.

Col 3, bar 5: turn(R), start turn on 'cut' (sq 1-n). At tip(L) (3-n), turn should be half-way and you should have your back to the audience. Turn is completed by da(R) sq 3, bar 6.

Next step starting at bar 7, col 3, and continuing to sq 3, bar 8, moves to the right. Right arm bent, elbow pointing diagonally upwards in direction of move. Left arm straight, palm facing down continuing the line of the right arm in the opposite direction. It must feel as if someone is pulling you along by your right elbow.

Col 4, bar 9, sq 1: R toe crosses in front of L. This step moves to the left and continues to da in sq 4, bar 10, col 5. As right leg moves across, left arm moves forward, right arm back. Arms opposite to legs until last da, then both arms are sideways just under shoulder height.

Col 5, bar 11: tapioca(R)–(L)–(R) then hop round left, arms out in gliding style.

Bar 12, sq 4: hop completes turn as tip(R) crosses behind. Body is slightly bent and hunched in, arms bent and fists clenched. This puts more emphasis on the leg movement. Watch out for the different timing from bar 13, sq 4.

Col 6, bar 15: slurp is written in sq before the actual beat as the slurp needs the time to make the step look effective. Arrow indicates direction the slide moves and the word 'slurp' is written in the lane of the sliding foot, the arrow is in the lane of the airborne foot. Both 'toes' land together in the sq immediately following the slurp, the landing being the actual beat.

Cols 7, 8 and first part of 9 is the brush step already fully covered on page 40.

Col 9, bar 23, sq 4-n: pu-he(L) movement is angled slightly left (10 o'clock) until bar 24, sq 2, he(L) body swivels with the three heels to face 2 o'clock.

Col 10, bar 25, sq 4-n: same step in opposite direction.

Col 11 is as it looks. Routine finishes at bottom of col 11, da(L). The following three squares in col 12 are the lead into a repeat of the routine, returning without a break in the rhythm, to the letter 'A' in column 1. You may repeat the routine as often as you like, but when you wish to finish, the final step is the da at the bottom of col 11, bar 30, sq 3. This routine has plenty of light and shade in it and the surer you are of the steps, the better you will be able to perform them. The answer then is *practise* – and *smile!*

Any of the tunes listed for Alpha-beat Routine or Time-step Saga would be fine for this one.

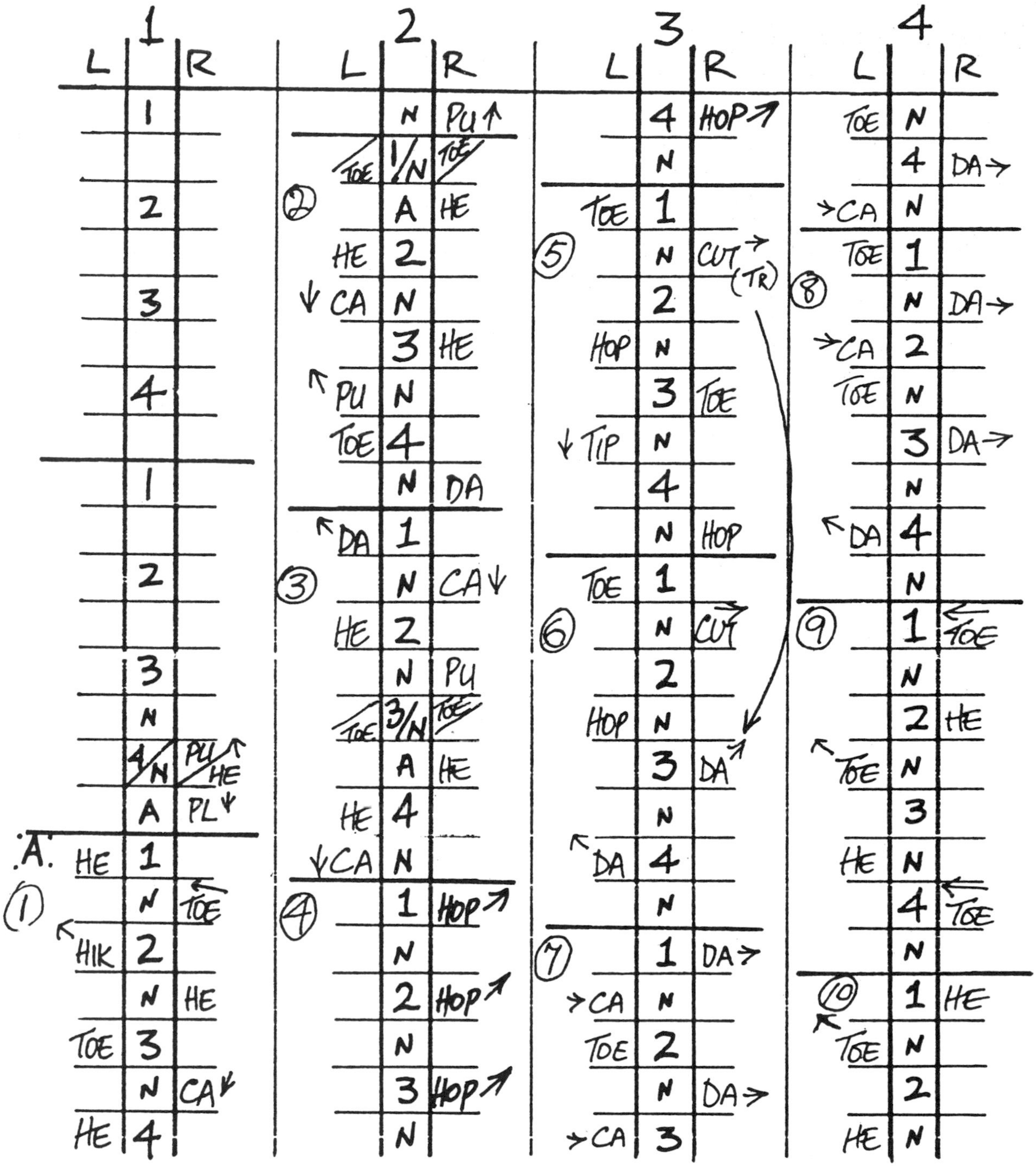

Fig 94a **Close beat feat** *(beginning)*

134

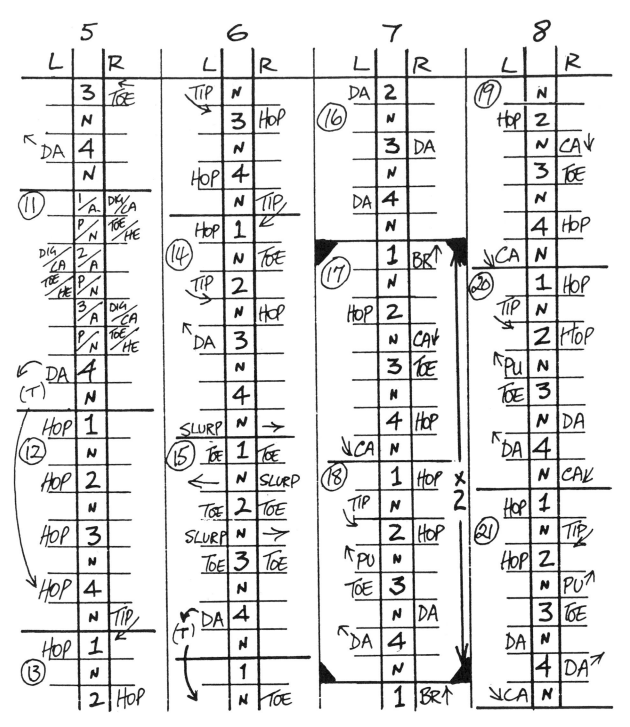

Fig 94b **Close beat feat** *(cont)*

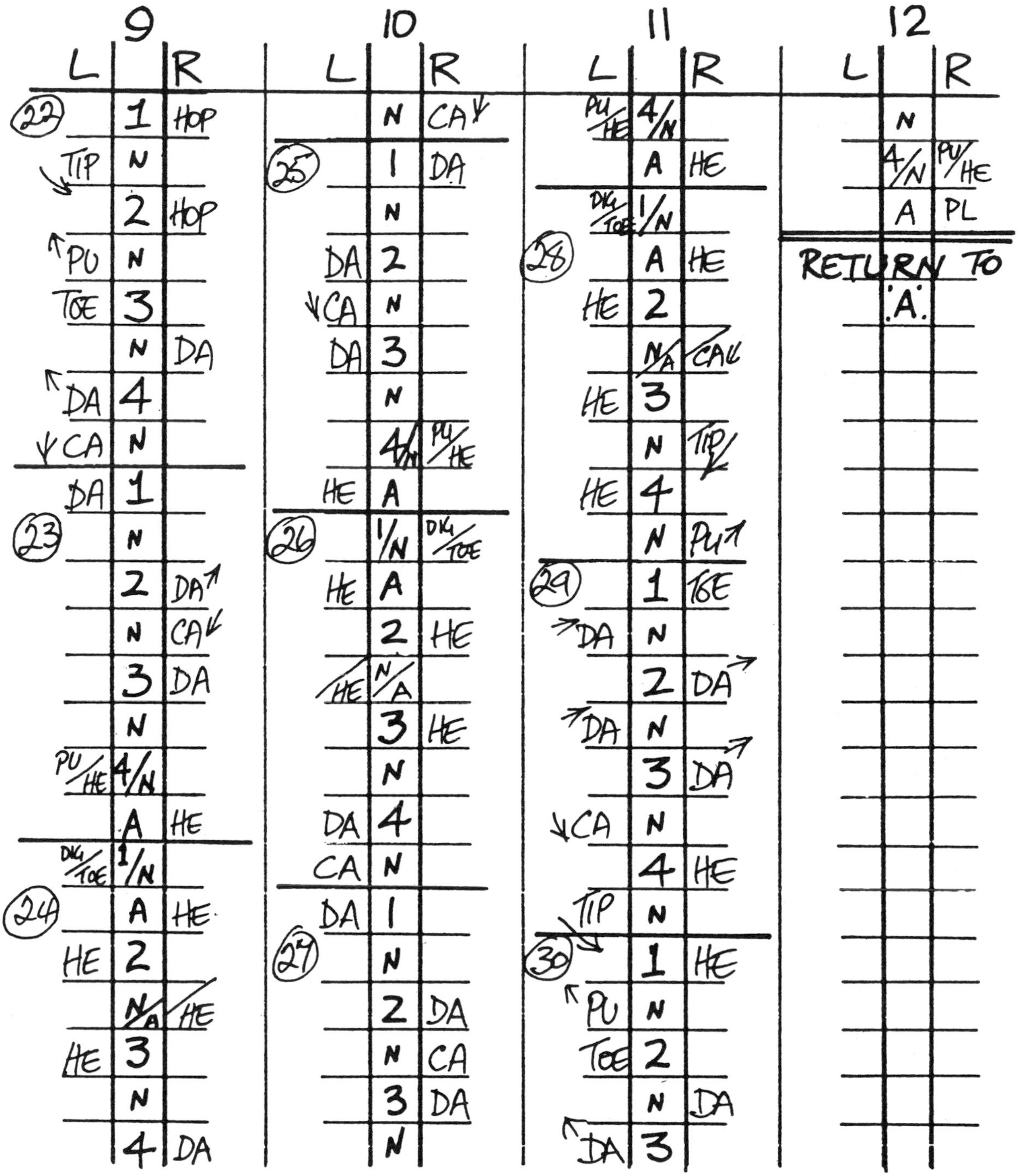

	9		10		11		12	
	L	R	L	R	L	R	L	R
(22)	1	HOP		N / CA✓	PU/HE	4/N		N
TIP↓	N		(25)	1 / DA		A / HE	A/N	PU/HE
	2	HOP		N	DK/TOE	1/N		A / PL
↑PU	N		DA	2	(28)	A / HE		
TOE	3		↓CA	N	HE	2	**RETURN TO**	
	N	DA	DA	3		N/A / CA	.A.	
↑DA	4			N	HE	3		
↓CA	N			4/N / PU/HE		N / TIP		
DA	1		HE	A	HE	4		
(23)	N		(26)	1/N / DK/TOE		N / PU↑		
	2 / DA↗		HE	A	(29)	1 / TOE		
	N / CA↙			2 / HE	→DA	N		
	3 / DA		HE	N/A		2 / DA↗		
	N			3 / HE	→DA	N		
PU/HE	4/N			N		3 / DA↗		
	A / HE		DA	4	↓CA	N		
DK/TOE	1/N		CA	N		4 / HE		
(24)	A / HE		DA	1	TIP	N		
HE	2		(27)	N	(30)	1 / HE		
	N/A / HE			2 / DA	↑PU	N		
HE	3			N / CA	TOE	2		
	N			3 / DA		N / DA		
	4 / DA			N	↑DA	3		

Fig 94c **Close beat feat**(*end*)

Flambée

This routine incorporates the flam, double-ca, tip, cutaway, four-side, a new toe-he flick, shunt hik, cutaway-ca, shim sham, cahito, the clapping step (page 90), da-pupl-ca, jump-o-foot (jut), slurp and finishes with shuffle-off-to-Buffalo. Add a few of the usual steps and we have quite a varied collection. The tempo is a fairly steady – four beats to the bar. As you become confident of the routine, you can raise the tempo to your own particular liking.

The first two bars are intro and the next two bars, marked 'toe', are intended to be a 'run-on' entry.

The routine starts with the flam(R), col 2, bar 1, then continues fairly simply through to bar 8, da-da.

Col 5, bar 8: double-ca starting with R foot. Bar 9 is as it looks. Also bar 10.

Col 5, bar 11: the tip-heels are fairly quick and need to be clean, arms in gliding position and head looking towards the (tipping) toe.

Col 6, bar 11, sq 3: as 'toe' is put down behind, L foot is raised in front in preparation for the cutaway in the next square. The da (sq 4-n) takes the weight as the R foot catches back and puts toe down.

Col 6, bar 12, sqs 2 and 3: the da-das establish equal weight balance and the sequence is repeated using the opposite feet.

Col 7, bottom sq: four-side. Hop on L foot whilst swinging the R foot behind.

Col 8, bar 17, sq 2: L foot hops again as R foot kicks out to the right. Sq 3: R foot returns to centre and drops as L foot is swung behind. Sq 4: R foot hops again as L foot is swung out to the left. Bar 18 repeats this sequence.

Col 8, bar 19, sq 1: this is a new movement and will need some concentration but is another worthwhile addition to the repertoire. The L foot is airborne out to the left from the previous step. Now it is put down as the start of a turn to the left. As you are half-way through the turn, the R toe is put down and takes the weight and, whilst still turning, the L foot catches toe and heel but remains suspended. The R heel is then dropped and the turn should be completed ready to step out again on the L foot (sq 4) repeating the step. The second turn should be completed by sq 2, col 9, bar 20. Da(L) toe(R) da(L) rounds off the sequence which is repeated on the opposite feet through bars 21-24.

Col 10, bar 25 sq 1: the shunt is directed towards 2 o'clock. The movement then travels backwards (8 o'clock) up to sq 4, bar 26.

Col 11, bar 27: the pu'he'pl (R) travels across the L foot and the 'toe' (sq 2-n) is put down across the front of the L foot which can then hik the R heel as it travels left. Sq 4: full turn left and continue moving left to end of bar 28.

Col 12, bar 29, sq 1: sequence repeated on opposite feet to end of bar 32 when we start the cutaway sequence. (cont on page 140)

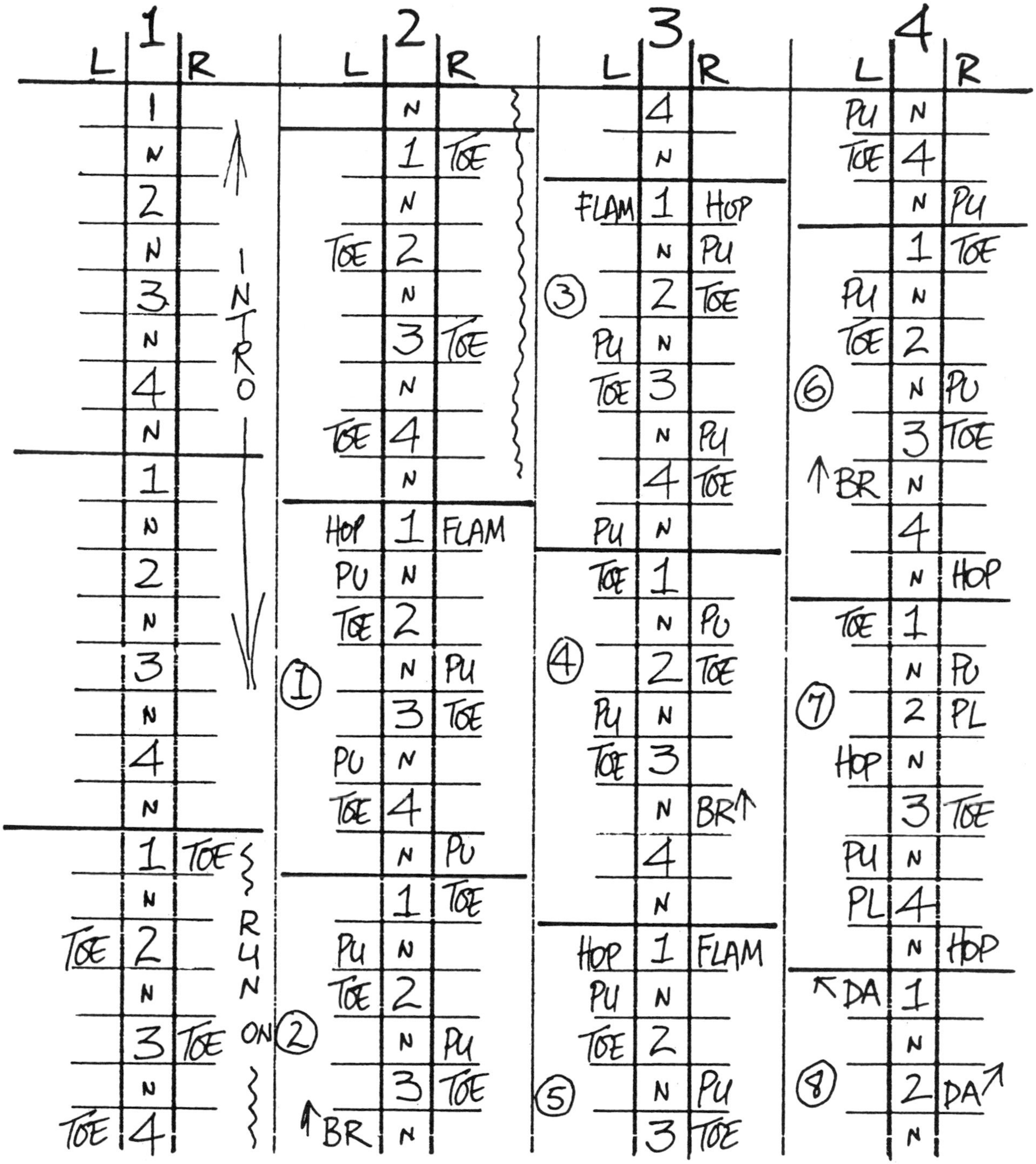
1 L R
1
N
2
N
3
N
4
N
INTRO
1
N
2
N
3
N
4
N
1 TOE
N
TOE 2
N
3 TOE
N
TOE 4
RUN ON
2 L R
N
1 TOE
N
TOE 2
N
3 TOE
N
TOE 4
N
HOP 1 FLAM
PU N
TOE 2
N PU
3 TOE
PU N
TOE 4
N PU
1 TOE
PU N
TOE 2
N PU
3 TOE
BR N
1
2
3 L R
4
N
FLAM 1 HOP
N PU
2 TOE
PU N
TOE 3
N PU
4 TOE
PU N
TOE 1
N PU
2 TOE
PU N
TOE 3
N BR
4
N
HOP 1 FLAM
PU N
TOE 2
N PU
3 TOE
3
4
5
4 L R
PU N
TOE 4
N PU
1 TOE
PU N
TOE 2
N PU
3 TOE
BR N
4
N HOP
TOE 1
N PU
2 PL
HOP N
3 TOE
PU N
PL 4
N HOP
DA 1
N
2 DA
N
6
7
8

Fig 95a **Flambée** *(beginning)*

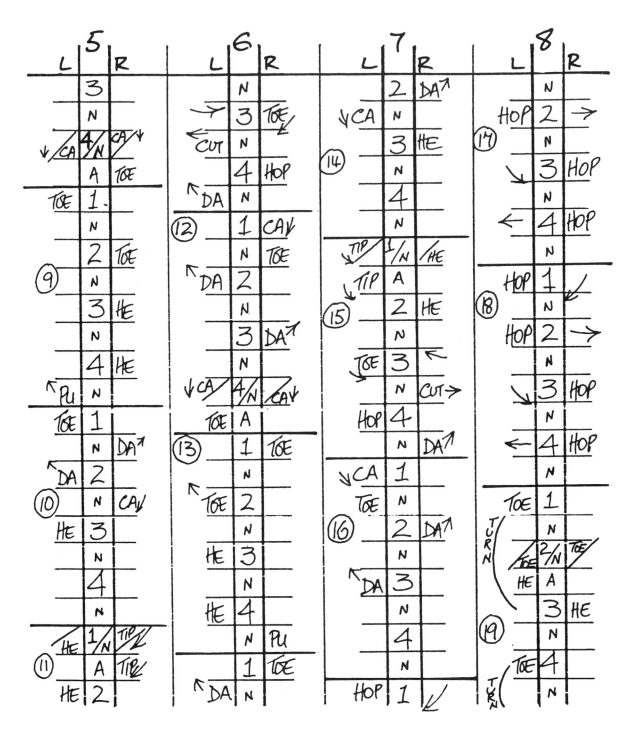

Fig 95b **Flambée** *(cont)*

138

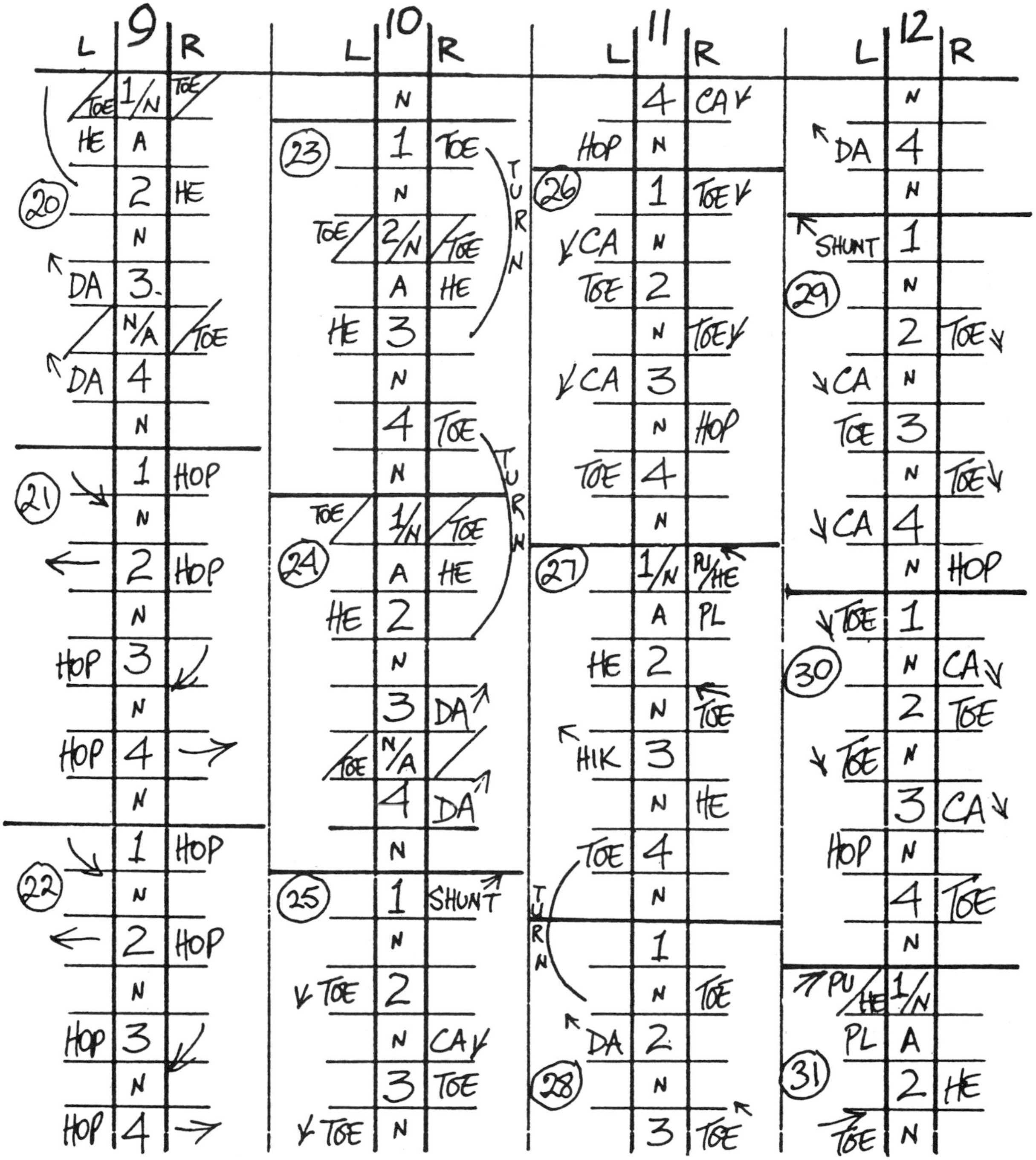

Fig 95c **Flambée** *(cont)*

Col 13, bars 33 and 34: cutaways repeated three times, then cutaway break (bars 35 and 36).

Col 14, bar 36, sq 3-n: the da(R) is in fact the first beat of the shim-sham routine which starts on bar 37 and continues into the cahitos half-way through bar 42 and ends on sq 3, bar 44.

Col 17, bar 44, sq 4-n: this is the clapping step explained on page 90. Start off facing left (9 o'clock). Bar 46, sq 4-n faces right (3 o'clock). Top of col 19 faces left again.

Col 19, bar 51: da-pu'pl-cas (page 38).

Col 20, bar 52: the claps are up in front of the face.

Col 20, bar 53: jump-o-foot (page 80) followed by slurps (page 78). Sequence repeated on opposite feet (bars 55 and 56).

Col 21, bar 56, sq 4-a-p-n(!): this hop pu'pl is snatched very quickly before leaning into the shuffle-off-to-Buffalo (page 97). Bar 57 is repeated including the 'snatch', then bars 58 and 59 are straight shuffle-off steps and your exit should coincide with the last beat of bar 59.

Any of the tunes listed for Alpha-beat Routine or Time-step Saga would be suitable for Flambée.

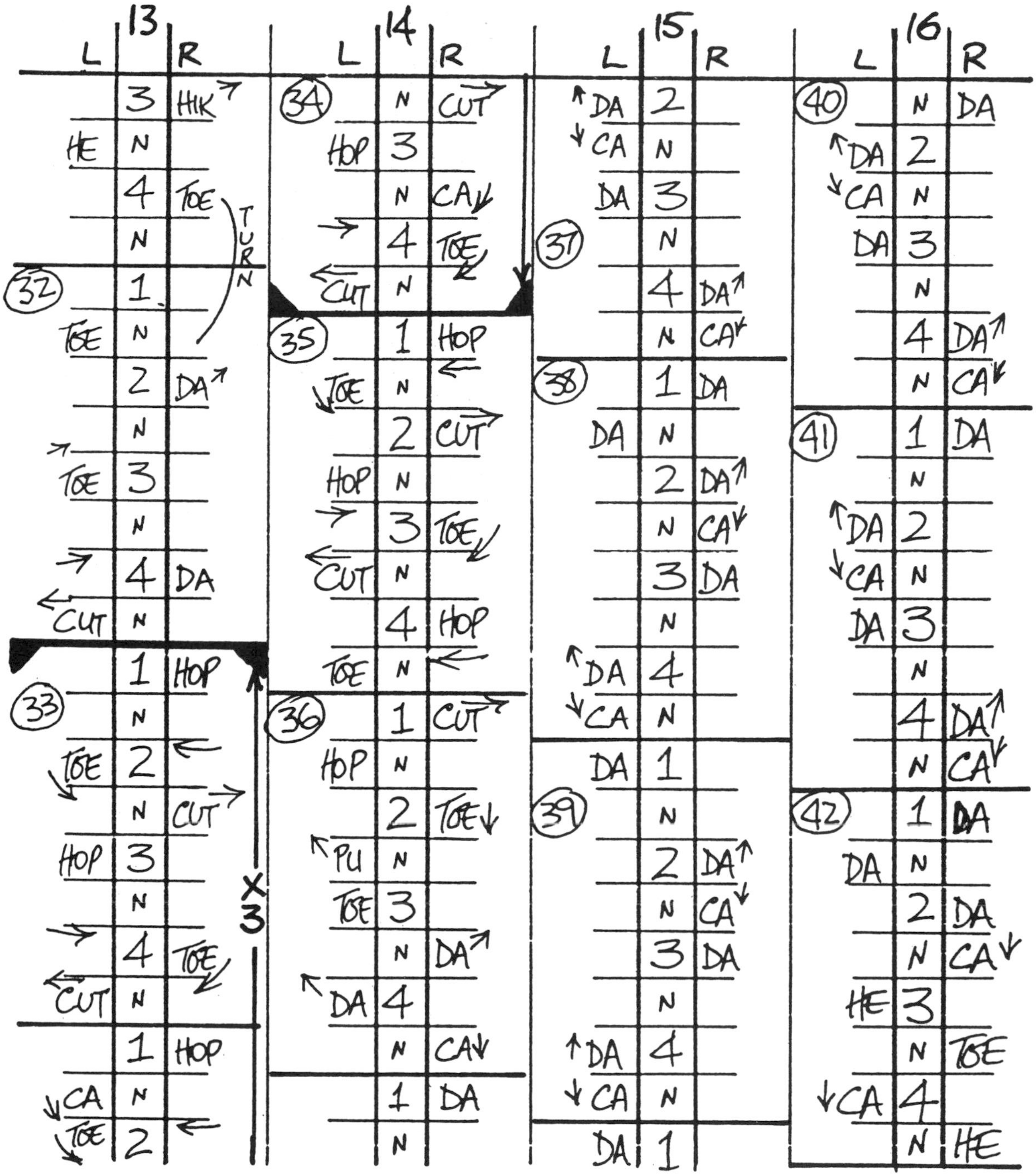

Fig 95d **Flambée** *(cont)*

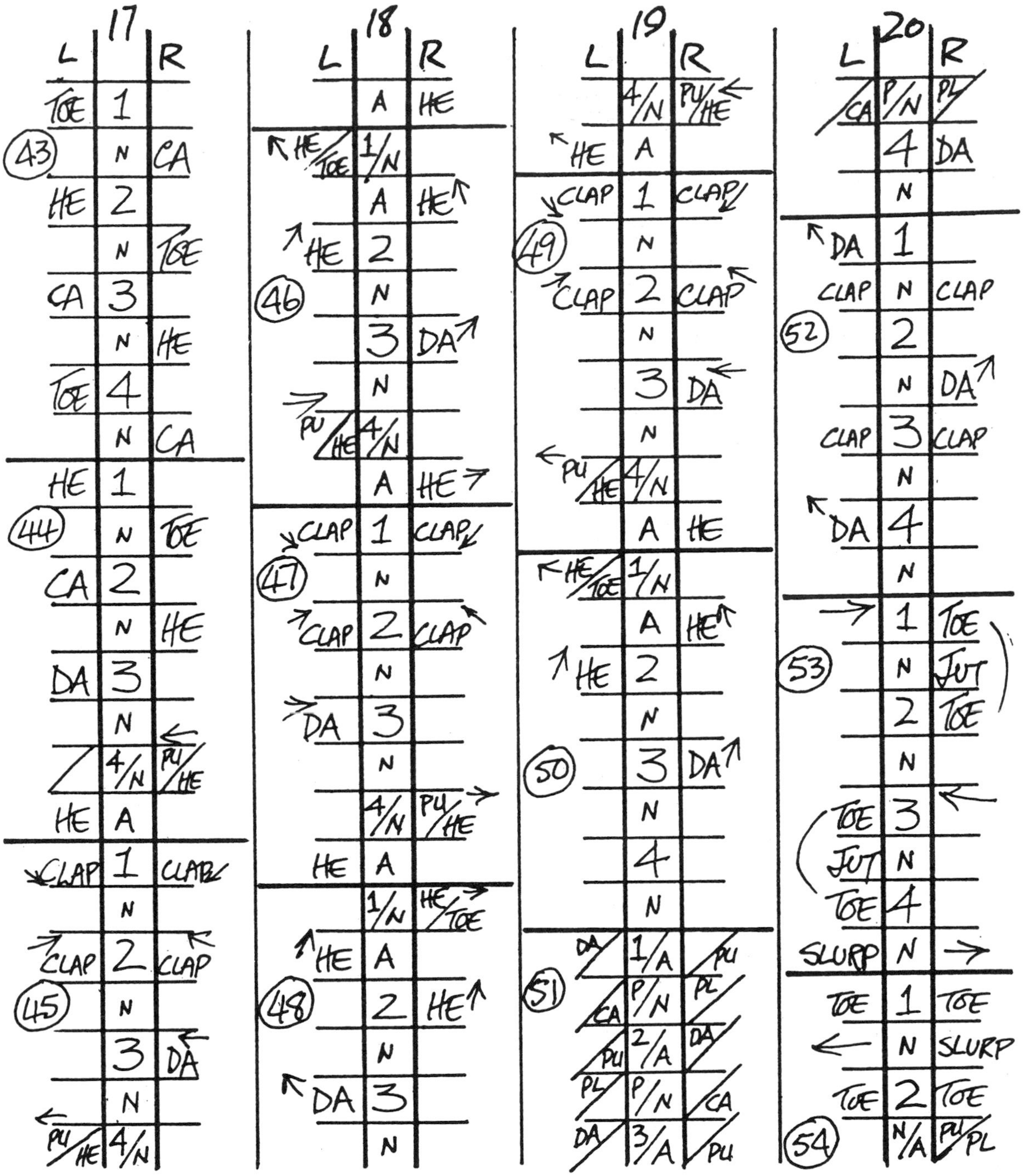

Fig 95e **Flambée** *(cont)*

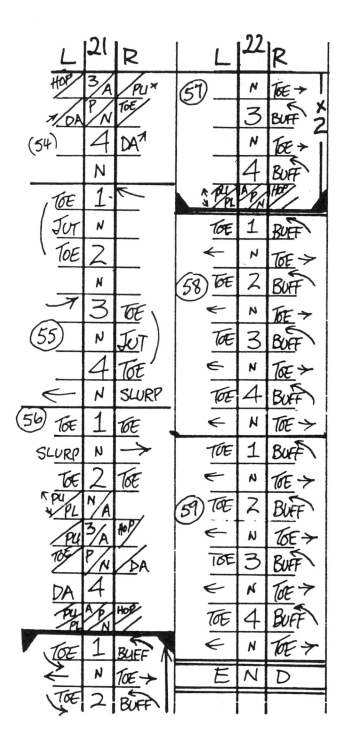

Fig 95f **Flambée** *(end)*